How to Dice an Onion

How to Dice an Onion

HACKS, TIPS, AND TRICKS FOR THE HOME COOK

ANNE SHEASBY

DOG 'n' BONE

This edition published in 2020 by Dog 'n' Bone Books
An imprint of Ryland Peters & Small Ltd

20–21 Jockey's Fields   341 E 116th St
London   New York
WC1R 4BW   NY 10029

www.rylandpeters.com

10 9 8 7 6 5 4 3 2

First published in 2007 by Ryland Peters & Small
under the title *Kitchen Wisdom*

A CIP catalog record for this book is available from
the Library of Congress and the British Library.

ISBN: 978 1 912983 15 5

Printed in China

Designer: Geoff Borin
Editor: Sarah Vaughan
Publishing Manager: Penny Craig
Publisher: Cindy Richards
Production Manager: Gordana Simakovic

Contents

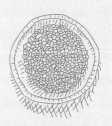
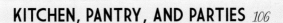

STAPLES

Storage Solutions

If possible, store foods on **NARROW SHELVES** so that you can easily see and reach items.

•

If you are short of space in the kitchen, cover the sink with a piece of wood cut to size or a large chopping board to create an **EXTRA WORK SURFACE** when the sink is not in use.

•

If you don't have a spice rack, put jars of **HERBS AND SPICES** in a rectangular basket or plastic box for easy access. Many spice jars only have the name of the contents on the side (designed to be viewed in a spice rack), so label the top of each jar as well, for easy identification.

•

Mount a key holder on your kitchen wall and use it to **HANG USEFUL SMALL ITEMS**, such as measuring spoons, small strainers (sieves), pastry brushes, and so on, within easy reach of your work space.

Stick the point of **SHARP** implements such as skewers and **KNIVES** into wine corks, to protect your hands when you reach into a drawer. The cork will also help to prevent the sharp edges from becoming dull.

•

Sturdy kitchen tiles make good **TRIVETS** for hot pans. Glue a piece of felt or cork on the back to prevent the tile from scratching your work surface.

•

Wine carriers or wine boxes are also useful for transporting food on a journey or **PICNIC**. Each compartment can accommodate a different food or drink.

•

Choose **STACKABLE CONTAINERS** to maximize storage space. Square or rectangular containers make better use of shelf space than round or oval containers.

•

Suspend a wooden or metal rail or rack from the kitchen ceiling and add large metal hooks from which to **HANG POTS, PANS, AND UTENSILS**. This will free up cupboard space and work surfaces.

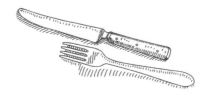

Use the space between two kitchen cupboard units to store **BAKING SHEETS**, chopping boards, trays, and similar items, to clear shelf space.

•

Hang a plastic shoe rack (with clear pockets) on the **INSIDE** of a kitchen cupboard **DOOR**, and store small items in the pockets, such as packets of herbs and spices, bouillon cubes, nuts, and gelatin (gelatine).

•

Use a **CARDBOARD WINE CARRIER** to store boxes of foil, plastic wrap (clingfilm), and similar shaped cartons upright in the slots. Store under the sink or in a cupboard to save drawer space.

•

A vertical metal file rack or plate drainer is an ideal way to **STORE CHOPPING BOARDS**, baking sheets, and pizza stones. Stored this way, they take up less space and it is easier for you to find what you need.

Containers

The **TOPS** of jars or bottles of food such as honey, jelly (jam), and maple syrup may become **STICKY**, making the lid difficult to remove. To prevent this, wipe around the rim and lid with a paper towel (kitchen paper) or a clean cloth (dampened in hot water) to remove any spillages, before replacing the lid. Alternatively, cover the top of the opened jar or bottle with a piece of plastic wrap (clingfilm) before screwing on the lid. This will help prevent the lid sticking.

•

To **REMOVE ODORS** from a container that you wish to use again, fill the container with hot water, then stir in 1 tablespoon of baking powder. Let it stand overnight, then wash, rinse well, and dry before use.

•

If you transfer foods from packets to storage containers, Scotch tape the food label onto the container so you can easily identify its **CONTENTS**. Make a note of the "use-by" or "best-before" date on the container, too.

•

MASKING TAPE is a great way of labeling containers. Simply stick a length of masking tape on the container and write on the tape. Fold over one end of the tape to create a tab, for easy removal. Also, every time you open a new jar or bottle, write the date on a piece of masking tape and stick it to the side of the container.

Save empty spice or herb jars with **PERFORATED LIDS** inside. Wash and dry them thoroughly, then use them to store flour, sugar, or confectioners' (icing) sugar. When you need a little flour to dust a work surface or sugar to shake over a cake, you will have it on hand.

•

Make your own flour or sugar **SHAKER** by carefully hammering a new nail through the metal lid of a clean, screw-top jar to make several holes. Put some flour or sugar in the jar, replace the lid, and you have a shaker ready to use.

•

If you are having trouble opening a twist-top jar or bottle, grip the lid wearing a **RUBBER GLOVE**, or use a rubber band or damp cloth instead. Alternatively, hold the lid under hot running water—the heat should expand the metal and make opening easier. Use a pair of nutcrackers to carefully grip and loosen small lids.

•

STORE FLOUR in its original sealed packaging or in an airtight container in a cool, dry, airy place. Ideally, buy and store small quantities at a time, to help avoid infestation of psocids (very small, barely visible, gray-brown insects) or pantry moths, which may appear in the cleanest homes. If you do find these small insects in your flour, dispose of it immediately and wash and dry the container thoroughly. Never mix new flour with old.

Food Basics & Taste Tips

If you run out of self-rising (self-raising) flour, sift together 2 tablespoons of baking powder with every 2½ cups (or 10 ml to 225 g) all-purpose (plain) **FLOUR**. This will not create quite such a high lift as self-rising flour, but it makes a good substitute.

•

Use **FRESHLY BREWED TEA** to add flavor and color to sweet and savory dishes such as meat casseroles and ice creams (using scented teas), and as the basis for fruit punches. Brewed tea can also be used to soak dried fruits for compotes, or for use in rich fruit cakes or fruit loaves.

•

Some raw fruits including **PINEAPPLE**, kiwi, and papaya contain an **ENZYME** that prevents gelatin (gelatine) from setting. However, they can be used in gelatin-set recipes if they are cooked first, as cooking destroys the enzyme.

Choose a reasonable quality wine for cooking, especially if the wine is not going to be heated, as in a fruit salad or syllabub. Cooking will not improve a **WINE** that tastes off or is inferior in flavor. Port or sherry can add extra flavor and color to casseroles, soups, sauces, fruit cakes, compotes, and other dishes.

•

GELATIN (gelatine) is commonly available as powder. Follow the package instructions carefully for use. As a guide to quantities, 1 sachet (about 11 g) of powdered gelatin or 3 sheets of leaf gelatin (depending on the size) will set scant 2½ cups (600 ml) of liquid.

•

Avoid adding **HOT GELATIN** (gelatine) liquid to cold mixtures, otherwise it will set on contact and form fine threads or lumps. Always add dissolved gelatin to a mixture that is warm or at room temperature.

•

ALCOHOL reduces the setting power of gelatin (gelatine). If you use wine in a gelatin-set recipe, heat it so the alcohol evaporates before you add the gelatin.

Leftover **CANNED (TINNED) FOODS** should be transferred to an airtight container, kept in the fridge, and eaten within 2 days. Once cans (tins) are opened, the contents should be treated as fresh food. This doesn't apply to ingredients sold in cans with resealable lids, such as cocoa powder.

•

To add flavor to dried **STUFFING** mix, add some chopped dried fruit, chopped nuts, lightly toasted seeds, or finely grated fresh Parmesan cheese before use.

•

To test the freshness of **BAKING POWDER**, mix 2 teaspoons with 1 cup (250 ml) hot tap water. If there is an immediate fizzing and foaming reaction, the baking powder can be used. If there is little or no reaction or a delayed reaction, discard the baking powder.

•

If you don't have a **PIZZA CUTTER**, cut a baked pizza into slices with clean kitchen scissors.

•

Store **COFFEE** (beans and ground) in the fridge or freezer, or it will go stale very quickly.

FLAVORINGS

Herbs

The best time to pick fresh **HERBS FOR FREEZING** or drying is just before they flower, when their flavor is at its most potent.

•

To dry herbs, hang small, freshly picked bunches in a warm, dry area such as near the stove. Once dry, store the herbs in **AIRTIGHT CONTAINERS**. Use them within 4 months of drying, or while still fragrant.

•

Chop **LEFTOVER** fresh herbs, spoon them into an ice-cube tray, top each portion with a little water, and freeze. Once solid, put the cubes in a freezer bag. Seal, label, and return to the freezer. Add the **FROZEN HERB CUBES** to soups, casseroles, and sauces as needed.

•

Use a **SALAD SPINNER** to wash and dry fresh herbs. It saves time and helps prevent the delicate leaves from bruising.

When substituting **DRIED HERBS** for **FRESH**, use roughly half the quantity the recipe calls for, as dried herbs have a more concentrated flavor.

•

If a recipe calls for snipped fresh chives but you don't have any to hand, try using a finely **CHOPPED** scallion (spring onion) instead.

•

To impart a **SMOKY** herb flavor to **GRILLED** (barbecued) food, scatter sprigs of fresh rosemary or thyme (soaked in water first to make them last longer) over the hot coals just before cooking.

STORAGE TIPS

Store all dried **HERBS AND SPICES** in a cool, dark, dry place. Spice racks filled with glass jars, unless they are in a cupboard, are not a good idea.

•

Store **FRESH HERBS** in the fridge. Wrap them loosely in an unsealed plastic food bag, or in a paper bag. Fresh herbs should keep well in the salad drawer for several days.

For a **HEALTHIER** diet, use fresh or dried herbs or spices to improve the flavor of many dishes, without adding extra fat or salt.

•

A fresh **BOUQUET GARNI** usually contains a couple of parsley stalks, a sprig of thyme, a bay leaf, and sometimes celery leaves and black peppercorns, tied together. To make one, either tie the herbs together with **KITCHEN STRING** (using bay leaves or a section of leek as the outer wrapper), or tie everything in a small piece of cheesecloth (muslin).

•

When preparing **FRESH BASIL**, tear the leaves rather than cutting them, as the sharp blade of a knife can easily bruise these delicate leaves.

•

Chopped fresh **HERB STEMS** (such as parsley stalks) are great for adding flavor to soups, sauces, and casseroles.

•

A quick and easy way to chop fresh herbs is to use **KITCHEN SCISSORS** to snip them directly into a bowl or over food, rather than using a knife and chopping board.

Spices

If possible, buy **WHOLE**, dried spices and crush them yourself, as required. **CRUSHING** your own spices ensures maximum flavor every time. Once spices are ground, they lose their flavor and deteriorate quite quickly.

•

Spices can be ground using a **PESTLE AND MORTAR** or in an electric coffee grinder kept specially for spices. As a general guide, replace ground spices (including those you have ground yourself) every 6 months.

•

Try mixing a pinch or two of ground spices such as curry powder, chili (chilli) powder, or turmeric with breadcrumbs or flour, and use this to **COAT FOODS** before sautéing.

•

Add ground spices such as cinnamon, apple pie (mixed) spice, or ginger to fruit **CRUMBLE TOPPINGS**.

•

A few gratings of **FRESH NUTMEG** will perk up mashed potatoes, cheese sauce, cooked spinach, and rice or semolina puddings. A little **GROUND ALLSPICE** will add flavor to mashed root vegetables such as rutabagas (swedes) and parsnips.

When making a **GOULASH**, try using **SMOKED PAPRIKA** instead of ordinary paprika. Smoked paprika will add a gentle heat, unique smokiness, and spice to the dish.

•

Ras el hanout, a Moroccan spice mix, will add flavor to many savory dishes, including **TAGINES** and other meat and vegetable dishes, **MARINADES**, couscous, and rice.

•

The color of a fresh chile (chilli) is no indication of how hot it will be. Most **CHILES** (chillies) are green when they are immature, ripening to varying shades of red. Generally speaking, the smaller and thinner the chile, the hotter it will be.

•

The **NATURAL OILS** in chiles (chillies) may cause irritation to your skin and eyes. When preparing them, wear disposable gloves or pull a small plastic bag over each hand, secured with an elastic band around the wrist, to create a glove.

•

Which is **HOTTEST**—chili (chilli) powder, cayenne pepper, or paprika? Chili powder and cayenne pepper are made from finely ground dried capsicums. Both are hot, but cayenne tends to be a little hotter. Paprika is made from ground dried **SWEET RED PEPPERS** and is generally milder and sweet in flavor. There are several types, including Hungarian paprika, which is hotter than Spanish paprika. Paprika from the USA tends to be mild.

To **REDUCE THE HEAT** of a fresh chile (chilli), cut it in half lengthwise, then scrape out and discard the seeds and membranes (or core).

•

To make **CHILE** (chilli) rings for garnishing, cut the stem end off a fresh chile, then insert a swivel vegetable peeler and rotate it inside to loosen the seeds and membranes. Shake any remaining seeds out of the chile, then slice it thinly into rings.

•

Use a melon baller to prepare fresh chiles (chillies). Cut the chile (chilli) in half lengthwise then, using the edge of a **MELON BALLER**, scrape down the inside of each half, removing the seeds and membranes as you go. Alternatively, use a small spoon or sharp knife instead of a melon baller.

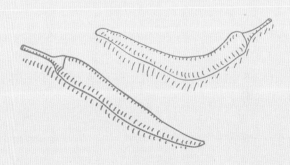

Other Flavorings

When buying **GARLIC**, choose plump bulbs with tightly packed cloves and dry skin. Avoid soft, moldy, shriveled, or sprouting garlic.

•

An easy way to prepare fresh garlic is to **GRATE** peeled **WHOLE CLOVES** on a fine or Microplane grater. This will produce finely chopped garlic ready for use.

•

Use a new, clean toothbrush to **CLEAN** all the little holes in a **GARLIC PRESS**, and to scrape off lemon zest caught in the teeth of the grater.

•

If you plan to **FREEZE** a recipe containing **GARLIC**, it is best to cook the dish without garlic, then add it to the food after defrosting. Garlic can taste musty when frozen.

•

If you have leftover **FRESH GINGER**, cut it into thick slices and freeze in a freezer bag for up to 1 month. Defrost, peel, and slice, chop, or grate as required.

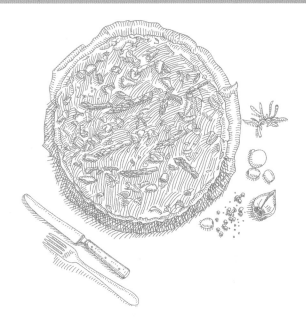

Use a metal **TEASPOON** to peel/scrape the skin off
a piece of fresh ginger.

•

To **GRATE** fresh ginger easily, peel a small portion at one end of
a large piece then grate that portion, using the unpeeled length
of ginger as a handle.

•

Use a garlic press to extract juice from pieces of fresh ginger.
Use the **GINGER JUICE** in salad dressings and sauces.

•

If a recipe calls for **FRESH GINGER**, do not use dried
(ground) ginger instead, and vice versa—the flavors are
very different.

To crush **BLACK PEPPERCORNS** coarsely, spread an even layer in a plastic bag. Seal the bag, dispelling the air inside, then bash the peppercorns with a rolling pin or meat tenderizer.

•

To bruise a stalk of **LEMONGRASS** and release its juices, bash the stalk with the back of a large sharp knife or a rolling pin, and use immediately.

•

Stir **WHOLE-GRAIN MUSTARD** into mashed potatoes or mayonnaise before serving to add extra flavor. Mustard also enhances salad dressings and sauces. A **PINCH** of powdered mustard added to cheese dishes will enhance the flavor.

•

Combine a little flour and **POWDERED MUSTARD**, season with salt and pepper, then rub over a joint of beef before **ROASTING**, to add delicious flavor.

If you add **TOO MUCH SALT** to a soup or casserole, add one or two peeled potatoes (cut into chunks) to soak up the salt, cooking them until tender. Discard the potatoes before serving.

•

Add nutritional yeast flakes to **VEGAN** and vegetarian dishes to add a savory cheesy, nutty flavor, or use as a condiment sprinkled over salads, soups, roast vegetables, pasta, and rice dishes. **NUTRITIONAL YEAST** is readily available in health food stores.

•

To remove the edible seeds from a **VANILLA BEAN** (pod), use a small sharp knife to cut the bean in half lengthwise. Starting at one end of each piece, press the knife down to scrape out the seeds, flattening the bean as you go. The empty bean can also be used as a **FLAVORING** in a sauce or added to sugar.

•

Pure **VANILLA EXTRACT** is an alcoholic extract of the vanilla bean (pod). The much cheaper imitation vanilla essence or flavoring has an artificial flavor.

Oils

Never fill a **DEEP-FAT FRYER** more than one-third full of oil (sunflower oil is a good choice for deep frying). Once the food has been added to the oil, the pan should be no more than half full.

•

Deep-fry foods in **SMALL BATCHES** and let the oil heat back up before adding the next batch. This will ensure that the food remains crisp. If too much food is deep-fried at one time, the temperature of the oil is reduced, so the outer coating will not be crispy. The food then absorbs fat and is less tasty.

•

For a richer-flavored **SALAD DRESSING**, use a nut oil instead of olive or sunflower oil.

•

Oil often **DRIPS** down the sides of the bottle. Make a thick cuff of paper towel (kitchen paper) and fasten it around the neck of the bottle with an **ELASTIC BAND** to catch any drips. Replace as necessary.

STORAGE TIPS

Store oils, **WELL SEALED**, in a cool, dark, dry place, away from direct sunlight. They can be kept in the fridge (though this is not necessary), but oils such as **OLIVE OIL** tend to solidify and go cloudy in the fridge. If this happens, bring the oil back to room temperature before use.

•

Buy oil in small bottles as it can become rancid if kept too long. **NUT OILS**, such as walnut or hazelnut, are the most unstable, so buy them in small amounts and use them up fairly quickly after opening.

Marinades

Marinades are used to add flavor to food and keep it moist, and to have a **TENDERIZING** effect. Meat, poultry, game, fish, shellfish, and vegetables can all be marinated. The marinated food is then cooked (with the exception of a few fish dishes, such as ceviche), often by broiling (grilling) or roasting.

•

When broiling, the food may be **BASTED** with the marinade during the initial stages of cooking, or the marinade can be reduced and thickened separately in a pan to make an accompanying sauce.

•

Many marinades contain an **ACID** ingredient such as lemon juice, vinegar, or wine, so always marinate foods in **NON-METALLIC** containers. Metallic dishes may react with the acid in the marinade.

•

An easy way to marinate **MEAT OR POULTRY** is to use a plastic food bag. Put the meat in the bag, add the marinade, and seal. Shake the bag, ensuring the meat is completely **COVERED** in the marinade. Once the meat is marinated, remove the meat and discard the bag. Never save and reuse marinades.

If using a raw meat marinade to make a **SAUCE**, make sure that the sauce is boiled before serving, to kill off any bacteria.

•

Plain (natural) **YOGURT** is sometimes used as a marinade as it contains active enzymes, which tenderize the food as well as adding flavor. One example of this is chicken tikka.

•

Spice rubs, simple combinations of spices, herbs, and salt, are used to rub over and marinate meat or **FISH** before broiling (grilling), roasting, or grilling (barbecuing). You can buy ready-made **SPICE RUBS**, or easily make your own using different mixtures of spices and seasonings, often ground or lightly crushed together using a **PESTLE AND MORTAR** before use.

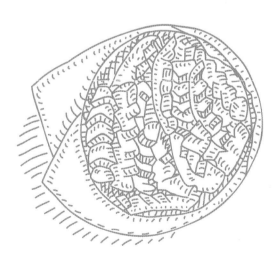

STOCKS, SAUCES, AND SOUPS

Stocks

When **MAKING STOCKS**, use a large pan with a pasta basket into which you can put all the solid ingredients. Once the stock is cooked, simply lift out the basket, leaving behind the **LIQUID** stock. Straining it is much easier without all the solid ingredients.

•

MEAT OR POULTRY stock requires long, slow simmering so that the maximum flavor can be extracted from the **BONES**. Fish stock is made quickly and vegetable stock can be made relatively quickly or slowly.

•

To **REMOVE FAT** from the surface of stock, pour the stock into a pitcher (jug) and add a few ice cubes. When the fat has set around the ice, lift it off, and discard.

Boiling stock tends to make it cloudy. To make a **CLEAR**, rich stock, simmer it gently over very low heat.

•

When making stocks, do not include **POTATOES** or potato peelings as they will make the stock cloudy.

•

PARSLEY STALKS are often used in stocks because they have more flavor than the leaves, and the leaves will turn bitter if cooked for a long period.

•

Do not add **SALT** to homemade stock. This allows you to control the amount of salt in any dish you make with the **STOCK**. Note that many ready-made stock products (cubes, granules, pots) are very salty, though reduced salt versions are readily available.

•

Use dried **SEAWEED** flakes as a healthy, vitamin- and mineral-rich alternative to salt when seasoning stocks, soups, sauces, and **STEWS**, or use as an alternative to **SPRINKLING** salt at the table.

•

Use the **WATER** in which **HAM** has been boiled to cook green vegetables, giving them a lovely flavor. You can also use the cooking liquid as the basis for **SOUP**, if it is not too salty.

When serving plain **RICE** as an side, cook it in a well-flavored **STOCK** (meat, chicken, or vegetable, depending on the main dish) rather than in water, to add extra flavor.

FREEZING STOCK

It is best to reduce stock by rapid boiling to get a **CONCENTRATED** stock for freezing. Frozen stock can be defrosted, or reheated from frozen, and it should then be simmered for at least 10 minutes. Frozen concentrated stock can also be diluted once defrosted, if desired.

•

Homemade stock can be frozen in **HANDY PORTIONS** for future use. Pour the cooled stock into the cups of a nonstick muffin pan (tin) and freeze until solid. Remove the frozen blocks from the **MUFFIN PAN**, put them in a freezer bag, seal, label, and freeze. Remove stock portions as you need them. Concentrated stock can be **FROZEN** in the same way, using ice-cube trays instead of a muffin pan.

Sauces

When making emulsified sauces such as **MAYONNAISE** or **HOLLANDAISE**, use a small blender or food processor to combine the ingredients. This will help prevent curdling or separation.

•

When making **EMULSIFIED SAUCES**, make sure all the ingredients are at room temperature. Mayonnaise may curdle if the eggs are used straight from the fridge.

•

When making an egg **CUSTARD** sauce such as crème anglaise, add 1 teaspoon of cornstarch (cornflour) to the eggs and sugar. This will help to stabilize the custard and reduce the risk of **CURDLING**. Once the sauce has thickened, cook it gently for slightly longer to remove the taste of the cornstarch.

•

Fine fresh **BREADCRUMBS** can be used to **THICKEN** some sauces and casseroles. Gradually stir the breadcrumbs in towards the end of the cooking time and simmer (adding extra breadcrumbs, if desired) until you have the thickness required.

Add a generous dash or two of **SHERRY**, Madeira, port, or red or white wine to gravy to add a rich and delicious flavor. Alternatively, stir in a little **HORSERADISH** sauce, mustard, cayenne pepper, or dried or chopped fresh herbs to add a more distinct flavor to gravy.

•

To boost a **CHOCOLATE SAUCE**, add a dash or two of whisky, brandy, or rum just before serving.

•

When a recipe calls for a sauce or stock to be **REDUCED**, an easy way to gauge this is to measure the depth of the sauce in the pan with a clean metal ruler. Work out from the present depth at what level the sauce should be when it has reduced as the **RECIPE** directs. Check the depth periodically as the sauce reduces, rinsing the ruler between dippings.

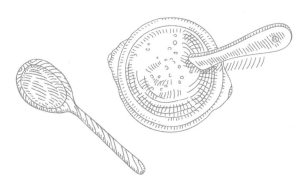

RESCUE REMEDIES

To rescue a **LUMPY** sauce or gravy, whisk it vigorously, using a wire (balloon) whisk, until **SMOOTH**. Alternatively, pour the lumpy sauce into a small blender or food processor and blend for about 1 minute, until smooth. You can also pour the sauce or gravy through a fine strainer (sieve) into a clean pan.

•

If an emulsified sauce such as Hollandaise begins to **CURDLE**, add an ice cube and whisk it thoroughly until smooth—the sauce should recombine. Similarly, if an emulsified sauce such as beurre blanc becomes **TOO HOT** during preparation, it will turn greasy and split. Whisking in an ice cube should rescue it.

•

If an **EGG** custard sauce begins to curdle or **SEPARATE**, strain it into a clean bowl, add one or two ice cubes and whisk briskly—the temperature of the sauce will be reduced, which should make it smooth once again.

•

To prevent a **SKIN** from forming on a thickened sauce (such as egg custard), cover the surface of the hot sauce closely with a piece of damp or lightly buttered (butter-side down) baking parchment or plastic wrap (clingfilm).

Soups

Save the **COOKING WATER** when boiling or steaming vegetables, and add it to soups, sauces, stocks, or gravies to add extra flavor and nutrients.

•

An excellent way of **THICKENING** soups is to stir in a little **OATMEAL**. It adds flavor and richness too. A small amount of instant mashed potato stirred in at the last minute is also a good way of thickening soup.

•

GROUND ALMONDS can add body to and enrich soups, as well as boosting flavor and texture. Add a small amount of ground almonds at a time to the blended soup (fish and chicken soups are ideal) and **HEAT GENTLY**, stirring, until the soup is thickened to the desired consistency.

•

A teaspoon or two of **PESTO** sauce stirred into each portion of a hot vegetable soup just before serving will liven it up.

•

For convenient **SINGLE SERVINGS**, freeze portions of homemade soup in large, thick paper cups or small individual containers. Remove them from the freezer as required, defrost, and reheat the soup thoroughly before serving.

•

GARNISH soups so they look attractive and complement the flavor of the soup. You could try chopped **FRESH** herb leaves or whole sprigs of fresh herbs; finely **GRATED CHEESE** such as cheddar or fresh Parmesan; crunchy croûtons (see following tips); finely chopped or thinly sliced blanched vegetables such as leeks, carrots, or zucchini (courgettes); cream, soured cream, or plain (natural) yogurt **SWIRLED** into the soup; finely chopped ham or crispy bacon; and finely shredded scallions (spring onions) or watercress.

•

For a **HEALTHIER** option, instead of sautéing **CROUTONS**, toss the bread cubes in a little olive oil and seasoning, then spread them on a baking sheet and bake in a preheated moderate oven (about 350°F/180°C) for 10–15 minutes, or until they are golden and crisp. For a taste boost, use **FLAVORED OIL** such as chile (chilli), herb, or nut oil.

•

For extra appeal when making croutons for soup, cut attractive **SHAPES** from the bread slices using small biscuit or jelly cutters, rather than cutting them into simple cubes. Toss the fried croûtons in chopped parsley just before serving, if desired.

•

Use **SPECIALTY BREAD** such as sun-dried tomato or herb bread to make croûtons. Whole-wheat (wholemeal) bread also makes good croûtons, and you can add a **CRUSHED** clove of garlic to the cooking oil for extra flavor.

•

Toss freshly made, warm croutons in a little finely grated fresh **PARMESAN** cheese, for extra appeal and flavor.

FRESH PRODUCE

Vegetables

Most vegetables keep best in the **FRIDGE**, but a cool, dark place is also good if you don't have enough fridge space. Potatoes should always be stored in the **DARK**, otherwise they will go green or sprout, making them inedible.

•

If you are vegetarian or vegan, when it comes to choosing your veg, make sure you eat all colors of the **RAINBOW**, and at least **FIVE PORTIONS** of a variety of fruit and veggies every day.

•

Starchy or floury potatoes make the best **FRENCH FRIES**. Their starchiness also makes them the best choice for mashed and roast potatoes.

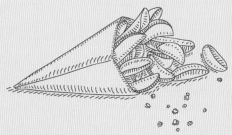

Don't use a food processor or electric beaters when **MASHING POTATOES** as this is likely to give them an unpleasant gluey texture. Use a potato masher, fork, potato ricer, or food mill. Once the potatoes are mashed you can beat them to lighten the texture, but this is best done by hand with a wooden spoon.

•

To clean **LEEKS** effectively, trim them, then slit them lengthwise about a third of the way through. You can then open the leaves a little and wash away any stubborn dirt from between the layers under cold running water.

•

Green leafy veg, such as broccoli, cabbage, kale, and okra, are good **PLANT SOURCES** of calcium for vegans. Dark green, leafy veg like watercress, broccoli, and kale are also a good source of iron. Add **GREEN** leaves to smoothies for a quick way to get your greens.

•

If you are preparing small onions for **PICKLING**, put them in a heatproof bowl and cover with boiling water. Leave for several minutes, then drain and cool slightly. The skins should peel away more easily.

•

An egg slicer is a quick and easy way to slice small **MUSHROOMS** (one at a time) or small cooked **BEETS** (beetroot) into thin, even slices.

One leg of an old, clean pair of pantyhose (tights) makes a good **ONION STORAGE** unit. Put an onion in the foot end, then tie a knot just above it. Add another onion and tie a further knot above, and so on. This keeps the onions separate and fresh during storage. Keep in a cool, dark place for several weeks.

To **ROAST (BELL) PEPPERS**, halve them and place cut-side down on the rack in a broiler (grill) pan. Broil (grill) for 10–15 minutes, or until the skins have blackened. Remove from the heat, cover with a clean damp kitchen towel, and let cool. Once cool, remove the skin, stalks, cores, and seeds and use as required. Alternatively, push a metal **SKEWER** lengthwise through the center of a (bell) pepper and hold it (using an oven mitt) over a gas flame, turning regularly, until blackened all over. Cool slightly, then rub off the skin under cold running water.

•

An ice cream scoop is an ideal way to **REMOVE SEEDS** and strings from vegetables such as squash and pumpkins without damaging the flesh.

•

To skin **TOMATOES**, score a small cross in the base of each one using a sharp knife. Put the tomatoes in a heatproof bowl, cover with boiling water, leave for about 30 seconds, then transfer them to a bowl of cold water. When cool enough to handle, drain, and peel off the skins using a paring knife.

Some recipes call for sliced and fried **EGGPLANTS** (aubergines). They absorb a lot of oil during sautéing, so try broiling (grilling) or baking them instead. Lightly brush the eggplant slices with oil and then broil (grill), or bake them on a nonstick baking sheet in a hot oven, turning once.

•

A pastry blender is ideal for chopping whole **CANNED (TINNED) TOMATOES** in a bowl. Alternatively, a pair of clean kitchen scissors can be used to snip the tomatoes into pieces while they are still in the can (tin).

•

Use a potato ricer to extract water from **COOKED GREENS** such as **SPINACH**. Alternatively, drain in a colander and press out excess moisture with a potato masher.

•

An easy way to **CLEAN MUSHROOMS** is to brush over them gently using a clean, soft toothbrush.

•

When baking stuffed (bell) peppers, keep them upright during cooking in the cups of a muffin pan (tin), or cook each one in an ovenproof **RAMEKIN** dish.

Keep **CELERY** and **SCALLIONS** (spring onions) fresh by standing them upright with the root ends in a pitcher (jug) or glass of cold water.

To minimize tears when **PREPARING AN ONION**, try peeling it under cold running water and leaving the root end intact when chopping.

•

To dice an onion, slice off the top, peel the onion (leaving the **ROOT** intact), then cut down in several slices almost to the root. Turn 90 degrees and repeat, still keeping the root intact. Carefully lay the onion on its side and **CUT** through in several slices, which will produce even-sized "dice." Discard the root.

•

Add a pinch or two of **SUGAR** to cooked tomatoes and homemade tomato sauce to maximize the flavor.

•

If boiling **SWEET POTATOES**, always cook them with their skins on and peel later, otherwise the white-fleshed sweet potatoes turn gray and the orange-fleshed variety go soggy.

•

JACKFRUIT provides a versatile "meaty" **ALTERNATIVE** (similar to a pulled-pork texture) for **VEGANS** and vegetarians. Easy to use, ready-prepped jackfruit is widely available in cans (tins) or packs (frozen and ready-prepped fresh are sometimes available, too).

Fruit

Choose **CITRUS FRUITS** with bright, uniform color that feel heavy for their size. Avoid those with shriveled or bruised skins. Always **WASH** (in warm water) or gently scrub and dry citrus fruits before grating, or choose unwaxed fruits.

•

To yield most **JUICE** from a citrus fruit, roll it under the palm of your hand on the work surface first. This also makes squeezing easier. Citrus fruit at room temperature also yield more juice.

•

If you need the juice and the **ZEST** from a citrus fruit, remove the zest first (you can freeze it in an ice-cube tray for future use) before squeezing the juice.

•

To chop sticky **DRIED FRUIT** easily, snip it into pieces with clean kitchen scissors or cut with a sharp knife dipped in hot water, lightly brushed with vegetable oil, or dusted with flour.

•

Hull fresh **STRAWBERRIES** using flat-ended tweezers, to avoid damaging the fruit and to prevent juice-stained fingers.

•

To **RIPEN** an **AVOCADO** or fruit such as a hard nectarine or peach, put it in a brown paper bag with a **BANANA** and keep at room temperature—ethylene released from the banana will hasten the ripening process.

To peel **PEACHES** or **PLUMS**, plunge them into a bowl of boiling water for 1 minute, then remove and plunge into cold or iced water to stop the **COOKING** process. When cool enough to handle, the skins will peel off easily.

•

A pineapple that has a distinctive, sweet scent will be ripe and ready to eat. Another test for ripeness is to pluck out one of the leaves—if it pulls out easily, the **PINEAPPLE** is ripe.

•

Rinse **FRESH BERRIES** such as raspberries, strawberries, and blueberries just before serving, as they will deteriorate quickly once washed.

•

To keep **SOFT FRUITS** such as raspberries, strawberries, and blueberries separate while frozen, **OPEN-FREEZE** them on baking sheets until firm before packing into freezer bags or containers.

•

Pit (stone) **CHERRIES** inside a plastic bag to prevent the juice from splattering everywhere.

•

Use a fork to remove red-, black-, and white **CURRANTS** from their **STALKS** without bruising them. Hold a few small sprigs at a time and gently comb through the stems with the fork, pushing the currants off as you go.

Dried **GOJI BERRIES** are a nutritionally-rich fruit, packed with vitamins, minerals, amino acids, and antioxidants. They can be eaten on their own, added to muesli or granola, trail mix, or **ENERGY BALLS**, or baked into snack bars and cookies (biscuits).

•

To prevent **APPLES** from splitting when **BAKING**, either cut a slit around the center or remove a strip of skin from around the stalk.

•

When making **APPLE SAUCE**, coarsely grate the apples rather than slicing or chopping them—they will cook faster and the sauce will be smoother.

•

APPLES and **PEARS** are less likely to break up during cooking if they are cooked in a **COVERED DISH** in a moderate oven, rather than on the stovetop.

•

Use a melon baller or a metal measuring teaspoon to remove the **CORE AND SEEDS** from halved apples or pears.

Salads

Keep salad greens **FRESH** by leaving them attached to their **STEMS**, if possible, and store in a plastic box or bag in the fridge salad drawer.

•

To dry salad greens thoroughly before adding dressing, use a **SALAD SPINNER**, then gently toss the leaves in a large bowl with a few sheets of **PAPER TOWELS** (kitchen paper). The paper should absorb any last drops of water.

•

DRESS SALAD greens just before serving, or they may wilt. Alternatively, serve the dressing separately.

•

When making **PASTA**, rice, or potato salads, add the dressing while the pasta, rice, or potato is still warm, so the flavors can be absorbed.

•

To make salad dressings or vinaigrettes, put all the ingredients in a clean screw-top jar, seal, and shake well. Alternatively, put the ingredients straight into the **SALAD BOWL** and whisk together well, before adding the salad.

•

For a tasty and creamy salad **DRESSING**, mash some **BLUE CHEESE** and stir it into mayonnaise, or a mixture of mayonnaise and plain (natural) Greek yogurt.

Soak **RAW ONION** rings in cold water for about an hour, then drain and pat dry before using in a **SALAD**. This helps prevent the onion flavor overpowering the salad.

•

Enhance salads by tossing in a handful or two of lightly toasted **SEEDS** or chopped **NUTS** just before serving. Good ideas include sunflower, sesame, or pumpkin seeds or linseeds, and hazelnuts, walnuts, pecans, or pistachios. Toasted seeds can also be sprinkled over cooked vegetables.

•

Nuts & Seeds

NUTS have a high **FAT** content so can turn rancid more easily if stored somewhere warm or damp. Buy nuts in small quantities, store in an airtight container in a cool, dry cupboard, and once opened, use them fairly quickly. Some nuts, such as shelled walnuts and **BLANCHED** almonds, also freeze well.

•

To blanch **ALMONDS**, put them in a heatproof bowl, cover with boiling water, and leave for 2–3 minutes, then drain and let cool. Rub the nuts in paper towels (kitchen paper) to remove the skins, or pinch each almond at one end and it should slip out of its skin.

To **SKIN** whole **HAZELNUTS** in a microwave, put them in a shallow dish and microwave on HIGH for 3–4 minutes or until lightly toasted, stirring every 30 seconds. Let cool completely, then rub in damp paper towels (kitchen paper) or a damp kitchen towel to remove the loosened skins.

•

To toast **SLIVERED (FLAKED) ALMONDS**, put them in a small skillet (frying pan) over moderate heat for 3–5 minutes or until the almonds begin to brown, stirring frequently.

•

To **GRIND NUTS**, process them in a blender or food processor until they are the consistency of fine breadcrumbs. Be careful not to over-process, or you may inadvertently end up with nut butter.

•

Before **ROASTING** or toasting whole **CHESTNUTS**, make a cross in the skins with a sharp knife to keep the nuts from bursting during cooking.

•

TOASTING SEEDS releases their natural oils and brings out their flavor. Ideal varieties include sesame, poppy, cumin, coriander, and mustard seeds. Sprinkle a thin layer of seeds over the bottom of a heavy-bottomed dry skillet (frying pan). Shake or stir the seeds over low to moderate heat until they are **GOLDEN** or release their fragrance.

Scatter sweet or savory muffins with a few **SUNFLOWER SEEDS** before baking, to add extra flavor and crunch.

•

Brush homemade or part-baked bread **ROLLS** with milk, beaten egg, or salted water, then sprinkle over some sesame, poppy, or caraway **SEEDS** before baking, for extra texture and taste.

•

A metal pastry blender is ideal for **CHOPPING** softer nuts such as walnuts or pecans in a mixing bowl. It saves the nuts from flying all over the place, which often happens when you chop them on a board.

•

If **MARZIPAN** or almond paste has become hard during storage, seal it in a plastic bag with a slice of fresh bread. The moisture from the bread should restore the marzipan to its pliable state.

DAIRY FOOD, EGGS, AND SUBSTITUTES

Butter

FREEZE freshly bought unopened blocks of **BUTTER** in sealed freezer bags, or wraped in foil. Salted butter freezes for up to 3 months and unsalted butter for up to 6 months.

•

When a recipe instructs you to **DOT** butter over the surface, use a coarse grater to **GRATE** chilled butter straight from the packet over the dish, or shave chilled butter over the dish using a vegetable peeler.

•

Instead of **RUBBING** butter into **FLOUR** using your fingertips, try coarsely grating chilled butter into the flour, then using a pastry blender or fork to work it in. This keeps the mixture as cool as possible. A **FOOD PROCESSOR** will also do the job quickly and easily.

If you need to **SOFTEN** butter **QUICKLY**, chop it into small pieces into a bowl at room temperature until it is soft enough to use. To soften in a microwave, put the (unwrapped) butter in a dish and heat on DEFROST (30% power) for 30 seconds for each stick (115 g) of butter, or until soft.

•

A melon baller is ideal for making **BUTTER BALLS**. Dip the melon baller in warm water first. Gently push each ball of butter out into a bowl of iced water (this will keep the butter balls firm). Store the butter balls in the iced water in the fridge until you need them. Drain before use or serve from the bowl.

•

When **SHALLOW-FRYING** with butter, add a little oil to stop it burning—butter browns easily and burns at a lower temperature than most vegetable oils. The mixture of butter and oil will give food a rich, golden color.

•

WRAP butter well or store it in a covered **CONTAINER** in the fridge, as butter picks up strong flavors from foods stored nearby.

•

When baking, use the **FOIL WRAPPERS** from blocks of butter or hard margarine to grease cake and loaf pans (tins).

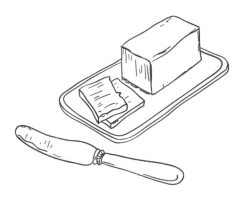

If you are **CREAMING BUTTER** for a cake mixture and it is slightly too cool, wrap a warm, damp kitchen towel around the bowl and continue to cream.

•

To make herb or **FLAVORED BUTTERS**, beat unsalted butter until softened, then beat in flavorings such as fresh herbs or **CRUSHED GARLIC** with a little lemon juice and seasoning until well mixed. As a guide, to make herb butter for 4–6, combine 1 stick (115 g) softened butter with 3–4 tablespoons chopped fresh herbs, 2 teaspoons fresh **LEMON JUICE**, and salt and black pepper. Turn onto a sheet of plastic wrap (clingfilm), shape into a log, and wrap in the plastic wrap. Chill in the fridge for at least 1 hour before cutting into slices to serve. **HERB** or flavored butters will keep in the fridge for 2 days or in the freezer for up to 1 month.

Cheese

STORE cheese in the fridge in a covered plastic container or loosely wrapped in baking parchment or foil. Do not wrap cheese tightly, as this prevents it from breathing.
Do not use plastic wrap (clingfilm), which can make cheese sweat, or waxed paper, which may draw the fat out and encourage mold.

•

Many hard or semi-hard **CHEESES** taste better **SERVED** at room temperature—remove the cheese from the fridge 1–2 hours before serving to enjoy it at its best.

•

GRATED hard cheese such as cheddar **FREEZES** well, but soft cheese such as Brie and most blue cheese (Stilton is an exception) does not. Grated cheese can be used straight from the freezer.

•

Use a **HAND-HELD** fine or Microplane **GRATER** when you need a small amount of a hard cheese such as fresh Parmesan. Grate directly over a dish just before serving.

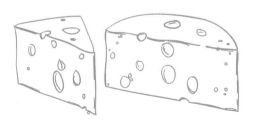

Use a vegetable or potato peeler to **SHAVE** fresh **PARMESAN** or other hard cheeses. Use a little pressure to make thin shavings and more pressure for thicker shavings.

•

Use an egg slicer to cut fresh **MOZZARELLA** into neat slices. Cut a standard mozzarella ball in half crosswise, then place one half in the **EGG SLICER**. Close the egg slicer to cut through the cheese, then remove the cheese and separate it into individual slices. Repeat with the other half.

•

It's easiest to **GRATE** cheese when it is **COLD**. Softer cheeses such as mozzarella grate most easily if you use a coarse grater with large holes. Alternatively, finely chop softer cheese rather than grating it.

•

When using **HARD CHEESE** such as cheddar, choose an aged variety and grate it **FINELY**, if possible. You won't need to use as much cheese to achieve the desired taste, so saving on calories and fat.

•

When making a **HEALTHIER** cheese sauce with reduced-fat hard cheese, remove the pan from the heat before adding the cheese to the cooked sauce to save it from overheating. Do this just before serving.

Hard cheeses such as cheddar, Gruyère, and Parmesan will **KEEP** for up to 3 weeks if stored correctly. Once opened, fresh, soft cheeses should be consumed within 3 days.

•

To keep **GRATED CHEESE** in one place, hold the grater and cheese inside a large plastic **FOOD BAG** while grating.

•

Combine grated reduced-fat hard cheese with fresh breadcrumbs, then sprinkle over the top of a baked dish and broil (grill) to create a **CRISPY TOPPING**. Reduced-fat hard cheese will melt under the broiler (grill), but it will not bubble and brown as its full-fat equivalents do.

Milk & Cream

Homogenized milk can be **FROZEN**. Whole milk that is not homogenized tends to separate on defrosting, so if you do freeze it, **SHAKE** it well before use once it has defrosted. Milk can be frozen for up to 1 month, and should be defrosted slowly in the fridge. Check the packaging for recommendations on storage and freezing.

•

Freeze milk in waxed cartons or plastic containers with enough room for expansion. Do not **FREEZE MILK** in sealed plastic bottles without pouring off some of the milk, or the container may split as the milk expands during freezing. Never use glass bottles, which will crack.

•

To help prevent milk from scorching during cooking, **HEAT** it gently in a heavy-bottomed saucepan or double-boiler. Rinsing the pan in cold water before adding the milk may also keep it from boiling over.

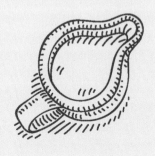

Cream can be frozen only if it has a **BUTTERFAT** content of 35% or more, so heavy (double), whipping, and clotted cream are suitable for freezing but light (single) cream is not. Light **CREAM** can be frozen if it is incorporated into a dish first. For best results, partially whip cream to the "floppy" stage before freezing it in plastic containers for up to 2 months. Defrost in the fridge overnight or for a few hours at cool room temperature.

•

Open-freeze piped **ROSETTES** of whipped cream before putting them in a sealed freezer bag. Arrange the frozen rosettes on your cake or **DESSERT** first, then let them defrost for 30–60 minutes at room temperature or 1–2 hours in the fridge.

•

To make cream into **SOURED CREAM**, stir 1–2 teaspoons of freshly squeezed lemon juice into ⅔ cup (150 ml) light (single) or heavy (double) cream. Let stand and the cream will thicken within 15–30 minutes. The heavy (double) cream will thicken more than the light (single) cream.

•

To achieve **MAXIMUM VOLUME** of whipped cream, add sugar or other flavorings (such as alcohol or pure **VANILLA** extract) to lightly whipped cream (when tracks begin to show on the surface), then continue whisking until the cream forms soft or stiff peaks.

When **WHIPPING CREAM**, chill the bowl and whisk beforehand, to keep the cream as cold as possible. Make sure the cream is well chilled too. Use a **WIRE (BALLOON) WHISK** rather than electric beaters—the cream will take a little longer to whip but there is less chance of over-whipping (for which there is no remedy).

•

To **PREVENT CURDLING** when adding plain (natural) yogurt (including Greek yogurt) to hot dishes, remove the cooked dish from the heat and stir in the yogurt just before serving. Do not bring the mixture to the boil again once the **YOGURT** has been added, or the yogurt will curdle.

•

DAIRY-FREE MILKS, such as oat milk, nut milks (e.g. almond, cashew, hazelnut), rice milk, soy milk, and coconut milk are ideal alternatives to dairy milk for vegans. They are readily available in supermarkets and **HEALTH FOOD SHOPS**, sold as long-life or chilled versions.

•

If you are a vegan, make your own dairy substitutes such as **NUT MILKS** (for example, almond or cashew milk), nut butters, cashew cheese, and coconut milk **ICE CREAM**, to save expenditure on ready-made versions, plus you'll know exactly what has gone into them.

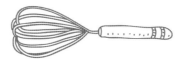

The creamy texture of **AVOCADO** flesh makes a great and healthy alternative to dairy foods in recipes such as smoothies or **SMOOTHIE BOWLS**, dressings, dips, mayo, salads, and sandwiches. It can also be used to make tasty **DAIRY-FREE** chocolate avocado mousse/pots.

•

Eggs

STORE eggs in their box in the fridge. Keep them pointed-end downwards and away from strong-smelling foods, as they can absorb odors through their **SHELLS**. Use by the "best-before" date.

•

Wash hands before and after **HANDLING** eggs, and discard any cracked and/or dirty eggs.

•

For many recipes, including cakes and pastry, eggs should be used at room temperature. Take them out of the fridge 30–60 minutes before using. Cold eggs may crack when you boil them, and egg whites at room temperature will whisk better than cold egg whites.

Freeze **EGG YOLKS**, first mixing them with a little salt or sugar (½–1 teaspoon per two yolks), in a covered plastic container for up to 3 months. **FREEZE EGG WHITES** in a covered plastic container for up to 6 months. Remember to include the number of yolks or whites, and whether they are sweet or salted, on the label. Once thawing, use on the same day and do not refreeze.

•

When **WHISKING** egg whites, always start with clean, dry, grease-free equipment. Grease, oil, or water in bowls or on whisks will prevent the whites from whisking stiffly. Plastic bowls are not recommended as the surface is difficult to clean completely of oil or grease; use a stainless-steel, glass, china, or ideally copper **BOWL**. Make sure the whites contain no traces of shell or yolks, which contain fat. If a little yolk has fallen into your egg whites, scoop it out, or touch the yolk with a piece of damp paper towel (kitchen paper)—the yolk should stick to the paper. For best results, use very **FRESH EGGS** and add a pinch of salt or cream of tartar at the start to help stiffen them.

•

Make an **OMELETTE** light and fluffy by folding whisked egg whites into lightly beaten egg yolks before cooking in the usual way.

If you like **FRIED EGGS** to look neat on the plate, break each one into a greased, round metal cookie cutter (2–3 inches/5–7.5 cm in diameter) in the skillet (frying pan). Alternatively, use a **COOKIE CUTTER** to trim the whites of fried eggs neatly.

•

If your baked savory **SOUFFLE** falls, just spoon or slice individual helpings onto plates and serve with a green or mixed salad. Serve a fallen sweet soufflé in spoonfuls, with whipped cream, ice cream, a berry compote, or fruit salad.

•

If you overcook **MERINGUES**, cool them, then crush and stir them into ice cream or whipped cream and mixed berries to make a quick dessert. Crushed meringues can also be used in place of **CHOPPED NUTS** to decorate the top and/or sides of cream-covered cakes and gâteaux.

•

If you overcook an omelette, let it cool and use it as a **SANDWICH FILLING**. Chop the omelette and combine it with mayonnaise and snipped fresh chives, if desired.

•

Chia seeds and flax "eggs" (made by combining ground **FLAXSEEDS** with water to make an egg-like binding agent), can be used to replace eggs in some **BAKING** and dessert recipes, providing a useful egg replacement for vegans.

MEAT, POULTRY, AND SUBSTITUTES

Meat

FRESH MEAT can be stored in the fridge for 2–3 days. Do not exceed the "use-by" date. If you buy meat from a **BUTCHER**, loosely wrap it in waxed paper or foil before refrigerating.

•

Add flavor to fresh **SAUSAGE MEAT** by kneading in some chopped fresh or dried herbs, or a little dried **STUFFING MIX**, before cooking.

•

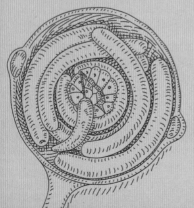

Cook sausages at a moderate temperature, as they may burst under high heat. Don't prick them before cooking, as this will allow the **JUICES** to escape.

Putting meat in the **FREEZER** for 30–60 minutes before **SLICING** makes it easier to cut thin, even slices as required for recipes such as stroganoff.

•

Produce even-sized **MEATBALLS** quickly by forming the mixture into a long log, then cutting off even slices and rolling into balls with wet hands.

•

SEASON MEAT just before broiling (grilling), or afterwards, otherwise the salt will draw out the juices and the meat will become dry.

•

When making a **SHEPHERD'S PIE**, beat an egg into the potato topping before covering the pie. Once baked, the pie topping should be tastier and browner.

•

Once a **ROAST** is done, remove it from the oven and let rest on a board in a warm place for 15–30 minutes (depending on size) before carving. This allows the muscles to relax and retain the juices within the meat, keeping it **TENDER** and making carving easier. Cover the resting meat loosely with foil to help retain the juices and heat.

When carving meat, cutting across the grain will give a more regular, **TENDER** slice, although it may be easier to carve the underside of some roasts, such as a leg of lamb, more thickly with the grain. Boned roasts are easy to **CARVE**, whereas meat on the bone should be carved in stages. Cold cooked joints of meat are much easier to carve than hot, and can be sliced very thinly.

•

When broiling (grilling), turn **CHOPS**, cutlets, and so on with tongs or spoons, to avoid piercing the flesh and losing their juices.

•

Add a square or two of dark or bitter **CHOCOLATE** to spicy meat dishes such as **CHILI CON CARNE**, to enhance the flavor and add richness.

•

If you don't have a roasting rack to fit your **ROASTING PAN**, sit the roast or bird on three or four tight rolls of foil, spaced slightly apart, in the pan instead. Discard the foil after use. Alternatively, **CELERY STALKS** or thick slices of onion make an edible roasting rack and will flavor the gravy.

•

If a cooked meat stew or **CASSEROLE** looks a little bland, stir in 2–3 teaspoons tomato paste (purée) to add body and color.

•

Tossing pieces of meat in flour before **SEALING** them helps to lock in the meat juices, as well as adding color to the dish. Flour also helps to thicken the **GRAVY**.

Tofu and **TEMPEH** give a "meaty" texture and provide a good source of protein for vegetarians and vegans. They are ideal **MARINATED** or served with a tasty sauce as they readily absorb or take on other flavors. **TOFU** is available in several types, the main ones being silken (soft), regular, firm, and extra-firm (firm tofu can also be bought smoked or pre-seasoned/marinated). Firm tofus are best for slicing and broiling (grilling), pan-frying, **STIR-FRYING**, deep-frying, baking, or kebabs, whereas the softer, creamy tofus, like silken tofu, are ideal for sauces, salad dressings, smoothies, dips, and even desserts such as cheesecakes, ice cream, and chocolate mousse.

•

Poultry

FRESH poultry will keep for up to 2 days in the fridge. Ideally, **FROZEN** poultry should be defrosted in the fridge and not at room temperature, to minimize bacterial contamination.

•

RAW CHICKEN can be slippery to handle. Use paper towels (kitchen paper) to hold chicken as you prepare it, or to remove chicken skin.

Use clean kitchen **SCISSORS** to cut away any excess fat or tendons from chicken breasts or legs.

•

When **ROASTING** a whole chicken (or piece of meat), put the bird or meat on a roasting rack in a shallow roasting pan to allow the **HEAT** to circulate around the meat and penetrate it more evenly.

•

To add flavor to a **WHOLE CHICKEN**, carefully lift the breast skin and push lemon or orange slices or small fresh herb sprigs underneath before roasting. Herb- or spice-flavored **BUTTERS** can also be spread under the skin before roasting.

•

For **CRISPY DUCK SKIN**, make sure the skin is as dry as possible before roasting. Prick the dried skin all over with a fork or skewer (but be careful not to pierce the flesh), then rub or sprinkle the bird all over with fine **SALT** and cook it on a rack or trivet in a roasting pan (to allow the fat to drain away).

•

Place a whole **LEMON** or peeled **ONION** inside the cavity of a chicken or turkey before roasting, to keep the bird moist and to impart subtle flavor to the meat juices used for gravy.

•

When **PAN-FRYING** chicken pieces, leave the skin on to give extra flavor and prevent the chicken from drying out. Remove the skin before serving, if desired.

To **FLOUR** pieces of chicken or meat, put the flour in a plastic bag, add seasoning, then add the chicken, a few pieces at a time, and shake until thoroughly coated. Shake off any excess coating before cooking.

•

Brush the skin of a whole chicken with oil, then sprinkle with **GROUND SPICES** (such as curry powder, cumin, or coriander), a spice rub mixture, or chopped fresh or dried mixed herbs before roasting to add flavor, color, and crispness to the skin.

•

When buying poultry, choose a bird that looks **PLUMP** rather than bony, with a creamy white or yellow skin (depending on the variety), without any sign of bruising, blemishes, or dry patches. Larger birds will be **MORE MEATY** and tend to have a more developed flavor.

•

To prevent chicken, meat, or vegetables from spinning around on **KEBAB** skewers during broiling (grilling), thread the pieces onto two skewers held side by side, slightly apart. This method also applies to shelled raw scallops.

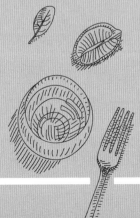

SEAFOOD

Fish

When buying whole fresh fish, look for bright, clear eyes, **SHINY SKIN** and scales, and red or bright pink gills. The flesh should be firm and the outer skin and scales should have a natural slime or film (they should not look dry). Fresh fish should smell fresh and clean. **SALTWATER FISH** should smell slightly of the sea, and should not smell strongly fishy or of ammonia. Fish with scales should have an even covering of scales with no large patches of loose scales. Your fishmonger should be happy to gut and scale fresh fish for you, if required.

•

When buying fresh **FISH STEAKS** or **FILLETS**, choose portions that are firm, plump, and moist, with a fresh, shiny, translucent flesh. Frozen fish should be bought tightly wrapped.

•

Check with your supplier that the fish you buy has not been previously **FROZEN**. If it has, do not refreeze it. Frozen fish is best defrosted slowly in the fridge overnight before cooking.

All fish is very **PERISHABLE** (especially once cut or prepared) and should be stored loosely wrapped or in a covered container in the coldest part of the fridge. Fish should be cooked and eaten within 24 hours of purchase.

•

Pluck out stray **BONES** from fish fillets using a pair of tweezers.

•

Choose **SMOKED FISH** that is plump and shiny, and avoid any that looks shriveled and dry. Avoid artificially colored or dyed fish if possible.

•

To **SCALE** a fish, grasp it firmly by the tail. Use a fish scaler, vegetable peeler, small sharp knife, or the back of a heavy knife and make short, firm strokes from tail to head to remove the scales, then rinse the fish.

•

To remove fishy odors after preparing fish, rub the cut surface of a **LEMON** over your hands, knife, and chopping board. Rubbing your hands with **VINEGAR** or salt, then washing them, will also help to get rid of the fishy smell.

•

When fish is cooked, the flesh becomes opaque and firmer. It should **FLAKE** with a fork and come away from the bones easily.

Before cooking whole (gutted) fish, tuck fresh **HERB SPRIGS** or **CITRUS FRUIT** slices into the cavity, so that the flavor penetrates the flesh.

•

Brush whole fish and fish **FILLETS** with oil before broiling (grilling) or **GRILLING** (barbecuing), to help prevent them from sticking to the broiler (grill) pan or grill (barbecue) rack. (This is also a good tip for meats.)

•

RAW FISH can be slippery to handle, especially when removing the skin from fillets. Use a folded paper towel (kitchen paper) to hold the tail end of the fish, skin side down, as you cut the flesh away from the skin using a sharp knife, working away from you. Alternatively, dip your fingertips in salt to help you grip.

•

When broiling (grilling) fish, turn it over using one or two lightly greased narrow **SPATULAS**. Try not to pierce the flesh as you will lose valuable juices.

•

To **SPEED** up the cooking process when broiling (grilling) or baking whole fish, use a sharp knife to diagonally **SLASH** the skin and flesh of the gutted fish at intervals on both sides before cooking. As the fish is cooking you will be able to see into the flesh to check if it is done. The slashes also encourage even cooking and add an attractive finish to the cooked fish. Brush the fish with a little **MELTED BUTTER** or oil during cooking if the flesh begins to dry out.

•

When **BAKING** fish steaks and fillets, brush them with oil or melted butter to keep them moist. Alternatively, add a **TOPPING** such as a breadcrumb mixture, chopped fresh herbs, lemon slices, or a sauce.

•

MICROWAVE ovens are ideal for cooking fish, as the fish retains all its delicate texture, shape, and **NATURAL JUICES**. Small and medium whole fish and fish fillets or steaks can all be cooked successfully in a microwave. Before microwaving whole fish, slash the skin in two or three places on both sides so that it does not burst during cooking.

•

To remove some of the saltiness from canned (tinned) **ANCHOVIES**, soak them in milk or cold water for 10 minutes, then drain and pat dry before serving.

•

To **FINELY CHOP** or mince canned (tinned) **ANCHOVIES**, press them through a garlic press to create a fine purée.

Store **SMOKED SALMON** in its original packaging in the fridge. Open it 30–60 minutes before serving. Wrap any leftovers, store in the fridge, and use within 2 days. Smoked salmon also freezes well for 2–3 months.

•

The longer **SALMON** is smoked for, the stronger the final flavor will be. Most smoked salmon is **OAK-SMOKED**, but **HEATHER-SMOKED** salmon is more aromatic, and **PEAT-SMOKED** may be sweeter and richer. Check the packaging to see what to expect.

•

Salmon **CAVIAR** (sometimes called keta caviar or ikura) is more affordable (and sustainable) than other caviars, but looks and tastes just as good. It is available alongside smoked fish in the chilled sections of some supermarkets, and is often used in **SUSHI**.

•

When removing a cooked large whole fish from the broiler (grill) or grill (barbecue), slide two lightly oiled metal spatulas side by side under the fish to give it support. This will help prevent the fish from breaking or falling apart. Gently lift the fish and transfer it to a **SERVING PLATTER**.

Shellfish

Once shellfish die, their flesh deteriorates quickly. Whether live or cooked, **SHELLFISH** should be kept refrigerated and used within 24 hours of purchase.

•

To de-vein large **SHRIMP** (prawns), cut along the back of each shell using kitchen scissors or a small sharp knife, and lift or scrape out the dark vein. Alternatively, use a skewer to pierce the flesh at the head end of the shrimp, just below the vein, then use the skewer to gently remove the vein.

•

When broiling (grilling) or grilling (barbecuing) shrimp (prawns) in their **SHELLS**, slit the back of each shell with fine scissors. When the shrimp (prawns) are cooked they will be easier to peel.

•

When buying **LIVE MUSSELS**, allow 9 oz–1 lb 2 oz (250–500 g) of mussels in their shells per person, depending on whether you are serving them as a starter or as an entrée.

To prepare fresh **MUSSELS**, fill a sink with cold water and add the mussels in their shells. Scrape off any barnacles using the back of a small knife, then pull away and discard the beards. Scrub the shells with a stiff brush or scourer, if necessary, to remove any **DIRT**. Discard any mussels with broken shells, or open mussels that don't close when tapped sharply on the work surface. Rinse and drain well. During cooking the mussels will open. Once cooked, discard any mussels that have not fully opened.

•

Choose **FRESH OYSTERS** with shells tightly shut. Fresh oysters will keep for up to 2 days in the fridge. Oysters that have been opened (shucked) are best eaten as soon as possible, but can be kept for up to 2 hours in the fridge.

•

When buying a live **LOBSTER**, choose one that is energetic and heavy for its size. Cooked fresh lobsters are easier to find—look for a firm, springy tail.

•

CRABS are bought alive or already cooked, in which case they may also be prepared, or dressed. When buying a live crab, choose an active creature. When buying cooked fresh crab, one that feels heavy for its size will contain more meat.

SCALLOPS may have been soaked in saline to make them appear bigger, but once cooked they will shrink to their original size. Look for scallops labeled "dry."

•

Scallops require brief cooking, usually 2–6 minutes, if broiled (grilled), poached, or sautéed, depending on their size and the intensity of the heat used. **DO NOT OVERCOOK** scallops or they will become rubbery.

•

To add flavor and to keep them moist, wrap **SCALLOPS** in strips of **BACON** (cut in half), then thread onto skewers and broil (grill) until the bacon is browned and the scallops are cooked and firm to the touch.

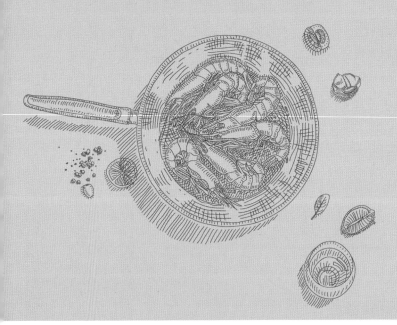

BEANS, GRAINS, PASTA, NOODLES, AND RICE

Beans & Grains

Store **DRIED** beans and pulses in airtight containers in a cool, dry, dark place. Make a note of the "best-before" date, and don't mix old and new beans. Older dried beans will take longer to cook than fresher ones.

•

Pick over and **RINSE** dried beans before use to remove any grit and debris. Spread dark beans over a white plate or chopping board to make it easier to spot any unwanted bits.

Beans and pulses are an economical, **LOW-FAT** source of protein, dietary fiber and a variety of vitamins and minerals, so if you are a vegan, keep your **STORECUPBOARD** stocked up with a variety of canned (tinned) and dried beans and pulses and eat them regularly.

•

With the exception of dried lentils and split peas, dried beans must be **SOAKED** before cooking. This helps the beans cook evenly and more quickly and makes them more digestible. If any dried beans float to the top of the bowl of soaking water, discard them as they may be damaged or moldy. Check the package instructions for soaking and cooking times.

•

After soaking, raw red **KIDNEY BEANS** and **SOYBEANS** (soya beans) should be fast-boiled for 10–15 minutes to remove harmful toxins they contain. Once fast-boiled, simmer the beans in fresh water until tender.

•

When cooking beans, never add seasoning until they are done. **SALT** toughens the skins and prevents the beans from cooking properly and softening. **ACIDIC** ingredients such as lemon juice, tomatoes, or wine, added to beans before they are completely cooked, will also toughen the skins.

•

Cook more beans than you need, then **STORE** the leftover cooled beans in an airtight container in the fridge for up to 2 days or in the freezer for up to 2 months.

Bulk out a pasta or rice **SALAD** by adding a can (tin) of drained and rinsed beans such as chickpeas, red kidney beans, black beans, or black-eyed beans. Alternatively, add some canned (tinned) or frozen corn (sweetcorn) kernels or cooked (cooled) frozen baby fava (broad) beans or peas.

•

When you are getting to the end of packets of **BREAKFAST CEREAL** such as cornflakes or bran flakes, crush the bits left using a rolling pin, then store them in an airtight jar and use as an alternative to breadcrumbs, for example for coating chicken or fish portions.

•

For added flavor, use good-quality **STOCK** (vegetable and chicken are ideal) instead of water to cook **COUSCOUS** or roasted buckwheat.

•

Quinoa (pronounced 'keen-wa') is naturally high in dietary **FIBER** and protein, and as a complete protein it contains all nine essential amino acids, so it's ideal for vegans and vegetarians. Available in two types, red or white, **QUINOA** is also **GLUTEN-FREE** as well as being a good low-GI food.

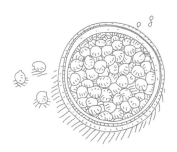

QUINOA is cooked in a similar way to rice and is a versatile alternative to rice and other grains. During cooking, the tiny, round, bead-shaped "grains" (actually seeds) expand in size to become fluffy with a slight crunch and a slightly bitter, **NUTTY** flavor.

•

Buckwheat, a grain-like, triangular-shaped seed (unrelated to cereal wheat) is wheat- and **GLUTEN-FREE**. It is available plain or toasted. If you are using plain buckwheat, you can lightly **TOAST** it in a dry skillet (frying pan) for a few minutes first, then use as required. **BUCKWHEAT** flour, flakes and noodles are also readily available.

•

Amaranth, a small **NUTRIENT-PACKED**, protein-rich, ancient "grain" (actually a seed), that is also gluten-free, is available as whole seeds, flakes, or flour. The whole seeds can be added to soups, stews, and salads (cooked first), or made into porridge, and the ground flour can be added to cakes and bakes.

•

Store "grains"/seeds such as quinoa, buckwheat, and **AMARANTH** in **AIRTIGHT** containers in a cool, dry, dark place.

•

Add a little **PEARL BARLEY** to soups and stews—it will add flavor and texture and have a thickening effect.

Use **OATS** or **OATMEAL** in crumble toppings in place of some of the flour to add flavor and texture, or use them to **COAT** fish or chicken portions instead of breadcrumbs before shallow-frying. Oatmeal or **ROLLED OATS** (ground in a food processor) can be used instead of some of the wheat flour in recipes such as breads, cookies, cakes, and stuffings, to add flavor and texture.

•

Cut cold, firm, cooked **CORNMEAL** (polenta) into different shapes (using a sharp knife or cookie [biscuit] cutters) before shallow-frying or broiling (grilling), to add interest.

•

Add flavor to cooked, hot cornmeal (polenta) by stirring in chopped fresh mixed **HERBS** or grated fresh **PARMESAN** cheese.

•

SEMOLINA can be substituted for some of the wheat flour in some cake and cookie (biscuit) recipes, to add a crisp, slightly gritty texture.

Use **MILLET** grain or seed (rinsed and drained) instead of rice to make a tasty and nutritious pilaf.

•

When **MAKING BREAD** in loaf pans (tins) or other shaped pans, grease the pan (tin) and sprinkle lightly with rolled oats, fine oatmeal, cracked wheat, wheat bran, or oat bran before adding the bread dough, then bake as normal. The baked loaf will have a lovely nutty-flavored **CRUST**.

•

SPRINKLE glazed homemade **ROLLS** or loaves of bread with wheat, barley, or rye flakes, cracked wheat, or fine cornmeal before baking, to add **DELICIOUS TEXTURE**. You could also try brushing the tops of store-bought part-baked rolls or loaves with a little salted water or beaten egg and sprinkling with any of the above before baking.

Pasta & Noodles

Small tubes and twists such as **FUSILLI** and **PENNE** are good for chunky vegetable sauces and some meat- and cream-based sauces.

•

Larger tubes such as **RIGATONI** are ideal for meat sauces.

•

Smooth, creamy, butter- or olive oil-based sauces and meat sauces are ideal for long strands such as **SPAGHETTI** (so the sauce can cling to the pasta).

•

LASAGNE, macaroni, and cannelloni work best when **BAKED** in recipes.

•

DRIED PASTA has a long shelf life and should be **STORED** in its unopened packet or in an airtight container in a cool, dry place. **FRESH** pasta is best used immediately. **LEFTOVER** cooked pasta should be kept in a sealed container in the fridge and used within 2 days.

•

Uncooked fresh pasta **FREEZES** well for up to 1 month, and can be cooked from frozen, allowing a little extra cooking time. Ordinary **COOKED** pasta does not freeze well on its own, but it freezes successfully in dishes such as lasagne and stuffed cannelloni.

For a **MAIN MEAL**, allow 3–4 oz (85–115 g) of dried pasta per person, or 4–5½ oz (115–150 g) of fresh **PASTA**. The same quantities apply to stuffed varieties of pasta such as ravioli.

•

Pasta must be cooked in a large volume of salted, **BOILING** water. Always add pasta to fast-boiling water and keep the water at a steady rolling boil throughout cooking. Once you have added the pasta to the boiling water, give it a stir, then cover the pan to help the water return to boiling quickly. Remove the lid once the water has started boiling again (to prevent the water boiling over), and stir occasionally. **FRESH** unfilled pasta takes 1–3 minutes to cook and filled 2–5 minutes to cook. When cooking dried pasta, check the instructions on the packet. When it is ready, cooked pasta should be **AL DENTE**—tender but with a slight resistance.

•

Do not rinse cooked pasta after draining unless it is being used in a cold dish, as rinsing will wash away the natural sticky starches that help the sauce cling to the pasta. If you are having **HOT PASTA**, drain it and serve immediately with the sauce. If serving pasta **COLD** (such as in a salad), rinse it under cold running water to stop the cooking process and drain it well, then toss with olive oil or salad dressing to keep the pieces separate.

Always serve hot pasta on **WARMED PLATES** or bowls,
as drained pasta loses its heat quickly.

•

For a **HEALTHIER** option and to increase your fiber intake,
choose **WHOLE-WHEAT** (wholemeal) or multigrain pasta
instead of white pasta.

•

Dried **NOODLES** (made from wheat and egg, rice, or mung bean
flour) need to be softened before use. This is done by briefly
blanching the noodles in hot or boiling water, or by cooking
them in boiling water for a few minutes. Fresh noodles
can usually be cooked without any prior preparation.

•

COOKED NOODLES are great for adding bulk, texture, and flavor
to warm salads and stir-fries. Noodles can also be added to
soups towards the end of the cooking time, to make
them more substantial.

Rice

UNCOOKED rice keeps well—store it in its unopened packet or in an airtight container in a cool, dry cupboard and keep an eye on the "best-before" date.

•

COOKED rice is a potential source of food poisoning. Cool leftovers quickly (ideally within an hour), then store in an airtight container in the fridge and use within 24 hours. Always reheat cold cooked rice until it is piping hot.

•

As an **ACCOMPANIMENT**, allow ⅓–½ cup (55–85 g) of uncooked rice per person, and for a rice salad or a **DISH** such as risotto, up to ⅔ cup (115 g).

•

Risotto, jasmine, glutinous, and **SHORT-GRAIN RICES** always stick together when cooked. For separate grains, choose an all-purpose long-grain or basmati rice.

•

Rice may be **RINSED** before cooking to remove tiny pieces of grit (if you buy it loose) or excess starch. Most packaged rice is checked and clean, however, so rinsing it is unnecessary and will wash away nutrients. **RISOTTO** rice is not washed before use, but **BASMATI** rice usually is—rinse it under cold running water until the water runs clear.

COOK rice in a **HEAVY-BOTTOMED PAN** with a tight-fitting lid and plenty of room, as rice triples in size when cooked. Use a fork to fluff up and separate the cooked grains just before serving.

•

Stir most types of rice once at the beginning of cooking, then do not **STIR** again until it is cooked. Stirring rice during cooking releases the starch in the grains and makes it more sticky. This is why **RISOTTO** rice is stirred frequently or continuously, to produce its characteristic sticky, creamy texture.

•

When **BOILING** or **STEAMING** rice, lightly toast the grains by sautéing in a little oil or melted butter for 1–2 minutes before adding the water or stock, to enhance its flavor. Add a generous pinch of crushed **SAFFRON** to the cooking water to impart a subtle flavor and yellow shade, or add chopped fresh or dried **HERBS** for extra flavor and color.

•

When making a **RISOTTO**, always use risotto rice such as **ARBORIO** or carnaroli, as they can absorb plenty of liquid without becoming mushy. Use a well-flavored **STOCK**. Remember that the stock should be boiling when added to the rice.

A couple of tablespoons of light (single) **CREAM** stirred into risotto just before serving adds extra smoothness.

•

For **RICE PUDDING**, always choose pudding rice, also known as short-grain rice, round or pearl rice, as this absorbs a large quantity of liquid due to its higher starch content, and becomes sticky and very soft during cooking.

•

To add **FLAVOR** to plain rice or semolina pudding, stir in the finely grated **ZEST** of 1 unwaxed lemon or 1 small orange before cooking.

BAKING

Bread

When **MAKING BREAD**, make sure the liquid is tepid (warm) or hand-hot. If it is too hot it will kill the yeast. If it is too cold, it will inhibit the yeast's action.

•

Never add **SALT** directly to **YEAST** as salt can inhibit its growth or even kill it altogether.

•

Use **CELERY SALT** or garlic salt instead of table salt when making savory bread dough, to add a subtle flavor to the baked loaf.

•

MEASURE ingredients **ACCURATELY**. Too much flour will result in a dry and crumbly loaf; too much liquid may give a dense, flat loaf. If too much yeast is used, the bread is likely to stale very quickly.

•

Don't be tempted to add too much **FLOUR** to the work surface when **KNEADING**, as this may make the dough tough and dry. A light sprinkling of flour should suffice.

STORAGE TIPS

Most homemade bread is at its **BEST** on the day it is made, or within 2 days of baking. Enriched breads (with a high fat or sugar content) should keep for up to 3 days. Many store-bought breads, especially sliced loaves, have a longer **STORAGE** life as they contain preservatives or flour improvers.

•

Store bread in a **COOL**, **DARK**, **DRY** place such as a bread box or bin. The cold temperature of a fridge will draw moisture out of the loaf, making it stale.

•

To keep a fresh loaf **CRUSTY**, store it in a paper or fabric bag. Wrap bread in foil or in a plastic bag if it has a soft crust.

To see if dough has doubled in size after the first rising and is ready for punching down (knocking back), gently insert a floured finger into the center—it should not spring back. Once the **DOUGH** has risen for a second or final time, press it gently with a floured finger—it should feel **SPRINGY** and **SOFT** and the indentation left by your finger should slowly fill in. This means it is ready for baking.

•

When **SLASHING** the top of a loaf before baking, use a sharp knife lightly sprayed with oil to ensure you achieve clean, **NEAT CUTS**.

•

PIZZA dough can be made and kneaded the day before you want to use it, then kept in the fridge in an **OILED** plastic bag, or in a covered oiled bowl. The dough will rise slowly overnight, and requires a quick knead before you roll it out. This slow-rising method can be applied to many yeasted bread doughs.

•

Prevent waste and **SAVE MONEY** by making leftover bread into breadcrumbs and storing in the freezer for up to 3 months.

•

If you have **LEFTOVER** toast or stale bread, bake it in a moderate oven until hard, then leave to cool and crush it with a rolling pin. Store the dried **BREADCRUMBS** in an airtight jar for up to 1 month.

Cakes

Always use the correct **SIZE** and depth of cake pan (tin) specified in the recipe. A smaller, bigger, or shallower pan may cause a cake to fail.

•

If you are **DIVIDING** cake batter between two pans (tins), it is important to divide the mixture evenly. Weigh the filled pans to check.

•

Most light cakes should be **TURNED OUT** of their pans (tins) a few minutes after removal from the oven. Rich fruit cakes are usually left to cool completely in the pan to allow them to solidify before storing and maturing.

•

Toss **DRIED FRUIT**, glacé cherries, and nuts in a little flour or ground almonds before adding them to a cake batter. This should prevent the fruit or nuts from **SINKING** to the bottom of the cake and keep them evenly dispersed during baking. If you wash the fruit, dry it well before using.

•

Create a **CRUNCHY TOPPING** for plain cupcakes by sprinkling them with granulated or coarse sugar before baking.

Store cakes in an airtight container, or wrap with foil or plastic wrap (clingfilm), and store in a cool, dry place. Wrap **RICH FRUIT** cakes in baking parchment before wrapping in foil, otherwise the fruit may react with the foil. Cream cakes should be kept in a covered container in the fridge.

•

Cut **SCONE DOUGH** into squares or triangles rather than rounds, so there won't be any trimmings to roll and you won't need a cookie (biscuit) cutter.

•

When making muffins, buns, or cupcakes, lightly spray the **PAPER CASES** with vegetable oil before use. They should then peel off more easily after baking.

•

If a cake **BREAKS**, stick the pieces together with jelly (jam) or frosting (icing), then ice or cover the cake with another topping.

Frosting & Decorating

To add a finishing touch to plain **SPONGE CAKES**, put a paper doily on top of the cake, then sprinkle with sifted confectioners' (icing) sugar or sifted cocoa powder. Carefully lift the doily off to reveal a **LACY PATTERN**. Alternatively, use strips of paper laid across the cake at intervals to create stripes or a lattice effect.

•

When tinting a **FROSTING** (icing), use a skewer or toothpick (cocktail stick) to control the addition of liquid food coloring. Dip the skewer into the bottle, then use it like a dropper. This also works well when you need to add a small amount of concentrated flavoring to recipes.

•

If you do not have a **PASTRY** (piping) bag, use a strong plastic bag. Snip a corner off the bottom of the bag, insert a nozzle, then fill with frosting (icing) and pipe as normal. Discard the bag after use.

•

Use the tines of a fork to draw **WAVY** patterns in **FROSTING** (icing), the back of a spoon to create **SWIRLS**, or the tip of a blunt knife to form peaks.

Pastry

Always **CHILL** pastry dough for 30 minutes before rolling it (then ideally chill it again for 20–30 minutes before baking). This helps to prevent excessive shrinking during baking, and also keeps the pastry from cracking when it is rolled out.

•

Stack **TRIMMINGS** of puff or flaky pastry on top of each other, rather than pressing them into a ball, before rolling them again. This will help to keep the important layers intact.

•

When making quiches or tarts, the edges of the **PASTRY CASE** should be flush with the rim on the pan (tin) or dish. When the pastry has been pressed into the pan, run a rolling pin over the top of the pan to break off any excess.

•

To cover a **PIE** with a pastry **LID**, lift the rolled-out pastry to the pie on a rolling pin and carefully unroll over the filling. Alternatively, fold the pastry into quarters, transfer it to the dish with the point in the center, then unfold.

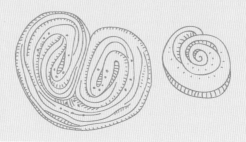

Brushing the base of an **UNBAKED** pastry shell with egg white or beaten egg will help prevent it becoming soggy. If you're baking a pastry shell blind, remove the beans and brush the base with egg 5 minutes before the end of the cooking time. An alternative is to brush a cold, baked pastry shell with a thin layer of melted **CHOCOLATE**. Let the chocolate set before adding the cold filling.

•

Toss **FRUIT** in a little flour (or flour mixed with ground spices) or cornstarch (cornflour) before filling a pie with it. The flour will help the juices thicken during cooking, which also helps prevent **SOGGY** pastry and juices leaking from the **PIE** during baking.

•

Place a sheet of foil or a large baking sheet on the shelf in the oven below a **FRUIT PIE**, to catch any drippings.

•

Cut two **SLICES** in a whole pie or cake before removing any portions. This will make it much easier to remove a neat and intact first slice.

•

When working with phyllo (filo) pastry, keep the **SHEETS** covered with plastic wrap (clingfilm). Otherwise, the sheets may dry out and crack, becoming brittle and unusable.

If you don't have a **ROLLING PIN**, use a straight-sided wine bottle instead. If possible, chill the bottle before rolling to keep the pastry cool as you work.

•

To prevent a **SOGGY** pastry lid on a pie and to keep it **CRISP**, cut a hole, cross, or several slashes in the top before baking, to allow steam to escape.

•

Use pastry trimmings to make **COOKIES** (biscuits). Gently knead in flavorings such as dried coconut and sugar, finely chopped nuts, chopped herbs and grated cheese, or poppy or sesame seeds, then cut into **SMALL ROUNDS** or shapes and bake in a moderate oven until crisp and golden brown.

Cookies

When making cookies, using **BUTTER** in the mixture tends to result in crisper cookies (biscuits) and margarine tends to make softer cookies.

•

To keep **BAKING PARCHMENT** in place on baking sheets when spooning out soft cookie (biscuit) dough, weigh the paper down in each corner with fridge magnets (remove them before baking). Alternatively, lightly spray the **BAKING SHEET** with sunflower oil before lining it with paper.

•

An easy way to transfer sticky **COOKIE (BISCUIT) DOUGH** to a baking sheet is to use an ice cream scoop. Dip the **SCOOP** into a bowl of cold water between each use to ensure an easy release of the dough. This also saves your hands getting messy.

•

When making a batch of cookies, double the quantity and make some for the **FREEZER** too. Place the balls, spoonfuls, or shapes of dough on a baking sheet lined with baking parchment. Open-freeze until firm, then transfer to a freezer bag or plastic container and return to the freezer. Bake from frozen, increasing the original cooking time by a few minutes. Most **COOKIE (BISCUIT) DOUGHS** keep well in a freezer for up to 1 month.

If baked cookies (biscuits) are **STUCK** to the baking sheet, return the baking sheet to the oven briefly—the cookies (biscuits) should then lift off easily.

•

Liven up plain sugar cookies (biscuits). Once baked and cooled, **DIP** half of each cookie into melted **CHOCOLATE** and let dry on a sheet of baking parchment. You can also top the melted chocolate with decorative sprinkles, finely chopped nuts, or dried coconut before letting set.

•

When baking more than one **BATCH** of cookies, once you remove each sheet of baked cookies (biscuits) from the oven, let the oven return to the correct cooking temperature before putting in the next batch.

•

If you have leftover **FROSTING** (icing), use it to sandwich together some cookies (biscuits) in pairs. Kids will love them.

•

To **CUT** cookie (biscuit) dough quickly, roll the dough into a long **SAUSAGE SHAPE**, then cut it into even slices using a sharp knife.

STORAGE TIPS

Many **HOMEMADE** cookies (biscuits) **FREEZE** well.
Seal them in freezer bags or pack in rigid, airtight, plastic
containers and freeze for up to 3 months. Defrost for
several hours at room temperature.

•

Do not store cookies (biscuits) in the same container
as **CAKES**—the cookies will absorb moisture from the
cakes and become soft.

•

If you place a **SUGAR LUMP** or two in a cookie (biscuit)
jar, this will help to keep the cookies crisp and fresh
for longer.

•

REVIVE soft cookies (biscuits) that have begun to
harden by placing a small slice of fresh bread in the
container with them.

SWEET THINGS

Desserts

For extra-crunchy **CRUMBLE** topping, replace about scant ¼ cup (25 g) of the flour with the same weight of chopped nuts, rolled oats, oatmeal, or crushed **AMARETTI** biscuits. Alternatively, sprinkle a loose, uncooked flapjack mixture over the fruit (do not press it down).

•

Make a **DOUBLE QUANTITY** of crumble topping and freeze half for next time. Break into small pieces and sprinkle it over the fruit before baking—there is no need to defrost it first.

•

To add a richer flavor to **PANCAKES** or crêpes, and to help prevent them sticking to the pan, stir 1–2 tablespoons of melted butter or sunflower oil into the batter.

•

When making dried **FRUIT COMPOTES**, use warmed fruit juice or scented tea (such as Earl Grey) for the soaking liquid, and add whole spices such as cinnamon sticks or star anise for extra flavor.

Instead of topping a **FRUIT PIE** with a solid pastry lid, lay pastry strips over the filling to create a **LATTICE** effect.

•

To make a crisper, browner **LEMON MERINGUE PIE** topping, sprinkle superfine (caster) sugar over the meringue just before baking.

•

To remove **SET** cold **DESSERTS** from their molds, briefly dip the mold in hot water before inverting the mold onto a serving plate.

•

AQUAFABA, the liquid in a can (tin) of chickpeas (that we tend to drain off), is an ideal egg (white) substitute for vegans. It can be whisked until thick, glossy and white and used to make things like **MERINGUES**, pavlova, mousse, mayo, and ice cream, or it can be used to lighten or add moistness to bakes such as brownies and muffins.

•

Ice Creams & Sorbets

Soften hard homemade ice cream in the fridge for 20–30 minutes before serving, to make scooping easier. Ice cream should not be allowed to **SOFTEN** too much and then be refrozen, as this will affect its texture and may cause food poisoning.

Save squeezed halved **ORANGES** or large **LEMONS**, with remaining flesh removed, to use as serving "cups" for ice cream and **SORBET**. Cut a small slice off the base, if necessary, to stabilize them. If you are not using them immediately, open-freeze them, then store in a sealed freezer bag in the freezer.

•

Ice **CRYSTALS** can form on the surface of opened tubs of ice cream. To help prevent this, cover the ice cream left in the tub with plastic freezer wrap or baking parchment, pressing it onto the surface before replacing the lid and returning to the freezer.

•

To make a quick **FRUIT SAUCE** ideal for serving with ice cream and sorbet, purée soft, ripe fruits such as raspberries, strawberries, peeled nectarines, or cooked blackcurrants, then press the purée through a nylon strainer (sieve). Gradually **WHISK** in sifted confectioners' (icing) sugar to taste and add a dash of fruit liqueur, if desired.

•

Serve **ICED DESSERTS** in chilled dishes to keep them cold when served, especially on hot days. Put the empty dishes in the freezer for a few hours before use.

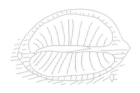

Sugar

Sometimes packed (soft) **BROWN SUGAR** becomes hard during storage, due to exposure to air. Add a wedge or two of fresh apple or a slice of fresh bread to the sugar container and the moisture should be restored within a couple of days.

•

If you need to use hardened brown sugar immediately, try **GRATING** it or blend it in a food processor to break it up.

•

Use a small, heavy-bottomed saucepan to make **CARAMEL**. This will allow the sugar to caramelize slowly, preventing the mixture from burning and sticking. If the caramel does stick to the pan, carefully add a little cold water and heat gently, stirring, until it has dissolved.

•

Pare long, thin strips of lemon, orange, or lime **ZEST**, bury the strips in a jar of white sugar and leave for a few days before use. The infused sugar can be used to add a delicate flavor to sweet recipes.

•

Bury one or two **VANILLA** beans (pods) in a jar of white sugar and leave for at least a week before use. The sugar will gradually absorb the flavor of the vanilla, and the beans will keep for a long time if stored this way. Use the vanilla sugar to impart a subtle flavor to cakes, cookies, and desserts.

Honey, Syrup, & Jelly

If honey or syrup hardens during **STORAGE**, stand the jar in a bowl of warm water for a few minutes or until the honey becomes liquid, rotating the jar occasionally. Alternatively, put the opened jar in a pan of water and heat gently, stirring the honey occasionally, until it is runny again. You can also heat the open jar in a **MICROWAVE** on HIGH for 10 seconds at a time, stirring between bursts, until the honey is smooth.

•

If you don't have a honey **DIPPER**, dip a fork into a pot of honey, twist it around several times, then remove and drizzle the honey as required.

•

When **MEASURING** sticky foods such as honey, syrup, or molasses, lightly spray the measuring spoon or pitcher (jug) with sunflower oil first. The sticky ingredient should slip out of the spoon or pitcher easily. Alternatively, use a metal measuring spoon dipped in hot water.

•

APRICOT jelly (jam) makes an ideal glaze for brushing over rich fruit cakes (such as Christmas cake) before adding marzipan, or for glazing fruit tarts. Put some apricot jelly in a small pan with a little water or **LEMON JUICE**. Heat gently, stirring, until the jelly has melted and combined with the water. Press through a nylon strainer (sieve) and use while warm. Cranberry or redcurrant jelly (jam) can be combined with a little lemon or orange juice, then warmed until smooth, and used as a glaze for fresh fruit tarts.

•

Maple syrup and agave syrup/nectar are good alternatives to honey for vegans. Other **SWEETENERS** like barley malt syrup and brown rice syrup may also be used in place of honey in some dishes.

•

Chocolate

Chocolate should be **WRAPPED** in foil and stored in a **COOL**, dry place—but not in the fridge, unless your kitchen is warm. If you do store chocolate in the fridge, wrap it tightly to avoid condensation, which may result in a harmless white "bloom" forming on the surface.

•

If you are **MELTING** chocolate and it seizes (becomes stiff and grainy), it has been overheated. Take it off the heat and stir in 1–2 teaspoons of vegetable oil, a few drops at a time, until the chocolate is smooth. However, if the **CHOCOLATE** is very scorched it may be unusable. Keep chocolate dry when melting it, as a single drop of water or steam will cause it to seize.

If you add a **LIQUID** to melted chocolate, warm it first, as cold liquid may cause the melted chocolate to solidify. Alternatively, add a small amount of liquid to **SOLID CHOCOLATE** pieces, then melt the chocolate and liquid together. If the chocolate seizes, add a little more liquid and gently heat and stir until it becomes smooth again.

•

To **GRATE** chocolate without it becoming sticky, use small pieces of well-chilled chocolate, brushing the grater with a dry pastry brush every so often. For best results, use a food processor. Grated chocolate can be frozen.

•

To make **CHOCOLATE LEAVES**, wash and dry some fresh, shiny rose leaves with a short stem. Brush several layers of melted chocolate onto the veined underside of each leaf and leave to set on a sheet of baking parchment. Once dry, carefully peel each leaf away from the chocolate using its stem. Store in an airtight container in a cool place.

•

To make chocolate **DECORATIONS**, line a baking sheet with baking parchment. Melt a little chocolate and put it in a paper pastry (piping) bag or small plastic bag, then cut the tip off the bottom corner. **PIPE** simple designs onto the paper. Let set, then carefully peel the paper away from the shapes.

To make fine chocolate **CURLS**, spread melted chocolate evenly over a cool surface (such as a marble slab) and leave until just set. Pull a citrus zester across the chocolate. For larger curls, pull the edge of a thin sharp knife at an angle of about 20 degrees through the chocolate. The chocolate should roll into curls or cigarette shapes. Alternatively, make shavings from a large **BAR OF CHOCOLATE** using a swivel vegetable peeler.

•

Pick up chocolate **SHAVINGS** with tweezers or a toothpick (cocktail stick) to position them on a cake or dessert — this way the chocolate won't melt in your fingers.

•

To shape chocolate **TRUFFLE** mixture into balls, use a melon baller dipped in hot water. Alternatively, coat your hands lightly with vegetable oil and roll the mixture between your palms.

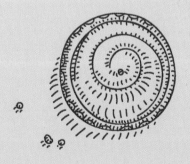

KITCHEN, PANTRY, AND PARTIES

Food Safety

Keep your kitchen **CLEAN** and **TIDY,** and disinfect counters after use with a mild detergent or an antibacterial cleaner. As far as possible, keep pets out of the kitchen.

•

Store food safely to avoid **CROSS-CONTAMINATION**. Keep food in clean, dry, airtight containers, always store raw and cooked foods separately, and wash utensils (and your hands) between preparing raw and cooked foods. Never put **COOKED FOOD** on a surface that you have used to prepare raw meat, fish, or poultry without thoroughly washing and drying the surface first.

•

Store **RAW MEAT** and **FISH** on the bottom shelf in the fridge to prevent it dripping onto anything below.

Never put hot food into a **FRIDGE**, as this will increase the internal temperature to an unsafe level. Cool leftover food quickly to room temperature, ideally by transferring it to a cold dish, then refrigerate. Cool **LARGE DISHES** such as casseroles by putting the dish in a sink of cold or iced water. Stir occasionally (and change the cold water often to keep the temperature low), then refrigerate once cool. During cooling, cover the food loosely to protect it from **CONTAMINATION**.

•

Don't use perishable food beyond the **"USE-BY"** date as it could be a health risk. If you have any doubts about the food, discard it.

•

Do not **OVERFILL** your fridge; if cold air cannot circulate properly, pockets of warm air may form as a result.

•

If non-perishable food is eaten after its **"BEST-BEFORE"** date (within reason), it should not cause any harm but its appearance, flavor, and texture may be past their best.

•

Store **LEFTOVERS** in airtight containers or wrap in plastic wrap (clingfilm) or foil, and keep in the fridge. Always eat leftovers within 2 days.

BACTERIA multiply quickly between 41–149°F (5–65°C), so food should either be kept or served cold or very hot. Ideally, the center of hot food should reach at least 158°F (70°C) for at least 2 minutes, to ensure that most harmful bacteria are destroyed. The internal **TEMPERATURE** of some cooked meats and poultry needs to reach a higher level than this, to be sure they are safe to eat. Meat thermometers or probes are useful for checking this.

•

REHEATED food must be **PIPING HOT** throughout before consumption. Never reheat any type of food more than once.

•

Raw or lightly cooked **EGGS** (found in homemade mayonnaise, some chilled mousses, soufflés, and other desserts, ice cream, sorbet, and egg drinks) are not recommended for people in higher-risk groups such as babies and young children, pregnant women, the elderly, and those who are ill or convalescing.

•

FROZEN meat and poultry should be thoroughly defrosted before you cook them, otherwise the center may not be cooked when the outside looks done, which could be dangerous.

Preserving

To sterilize **JARS**, wash them in hot, soapy water, then rinse well (or give them a hot wash in the dishwasher). Heat the jars upside-down in a low oven—they must be clean, dry, and warm when you add the hot preserve.

•

FILL each jar with the hot preserve, then cover with a waxed disc and seal with a clean lid. Do this immediately to prevent moisture collecting under the lids and encouraging mold. Leave to cool before labeling, then store in a cool, dry, dark place.

•

Use a wide, heavy-bottomed non-reactive stainless steel, aluminum, or enameled cast-iron pan to cook **PRESERVES**. Traditional copper or brass pans can be used for jellies (jams) and preserves, but they are not suitable for soaking fruits or making pickles or **CHUTNEYS** containing acidic ingredients like vinegar, as the acid may corrode the metal.

•

Choose **FRUIT** that is just ripe or slightly under-ripe for jellies (jams) and preserves, as this will contain the most **PECTIN**, which is needed to make the jam set properly. Overripe fruit contains much less pectin. Pectin content varies greatly from one type of fruit to another.

Warm a candy (sugar) **THERMOMETER** in hot water before use to prevent it from cracking.

•

When making jelly (jam) with cherries, plums, or other **STONE FRUITS**, wash the fruit before use, but don't remove the pits (stones). Once the jelly is boiling, the pits will float to the surface and can be skimmed off, saving you time.

•

Don't fill preserving pans more than half full, to prevent the hot jelly (jam) from **BOILING OVER** or splashing too much.

•

Once the sugar has dissolved in your jelly (jam) but before it boils, add a tablespoon of unsalted **BUTTER** to reduce scum on the surface.

•

Warm the sugar before adding it to the **SOFTENED FRUIT**, so that it will dissolve quickly and help give a clear set to sweet preserves.

•

When making jelly (jam) or marmalade with pieces of **WHOLE FRUIT**, let the jelly stand for 15 minutes once cooked. When the mixture has begun to set, stir it to distribute the fruit or peel

evenly, then ladle into sterilized jars. This should help prevent the fruit or peel from **RISING** to the top of the jars when fully set.

•

If your chosen jelly (jam) fruit has a **LOWER PECTIN** content, such as strawberries, peaches, or rhubarb, use jelling (jam) sugar (ordinary **CANE SUGAR** to which natural apple pectin or citric acid is added), or add lemon juice and liquid or powdered pectin. Alternatively, combine a lower-pectin fruit with a high-pectin fruit, such as strawberries with raspberries.

•

Long, slow cooking is best for **CHUTNEYS**, so the ingredients can soften and combine to create the maximum flavor and ideal texture.

•

STORE chutneys, pickles, and relishes for at least 1 month (preferably 2–3 months) before eating, to allow the flavors to **DEVELOP**.

Freezing

Freeze food that is in prime condition, on the day of purchase, or as soon as a dish is made and cooled. **FREEZE** food **QUICKLY** and in small quantities, if possible. Label and date food and keep a good rotation of stock in the freezer.

•

Always leave a gap in the container when freezing liquids, so that there is enough room for the liquid to **EXPAND** as it freezes.

•

Always let food **COOL** before freezing. Warm or hot food will increase the internal temperature of the freezer and may cause other foods to begin to defrost and spoil.

•

It is important to **DEFROST** food slowly, as rapid defrosting can lead to moisture loss and dry, tasteless food. Defrosting overnight or for several hours in the fridge is ideal. Cover food loosely while it is defrosting. Do not refreeze food once it has defrosted.

When freezing items such as burgers or chops, **STACK** them with a piece of waxed or baking parchment between each one, then put them in freezer bags and freeze for up to 2 months. You can then remove **INDIVIDUAL PORTIONS** as needed.

•

Freeze leftover **WINE** in an ice-cube tray. Once solid, transfer the wine cubes to a freezer bag. The wine cubes can be added to casseroles, stews, and gravies for extra flavor.

•

Handle food to be frozen as little as possible and keep everything **CLEAN**. Freezing does not kill bacteria or germs.

•

If the **POWER** of your freezer goes off, prevent warm air entering by keeping the door closed. Wrap the freezer in a blanket if possible to increase insulation, but do not cover the condenser or pipes at the rear. The food should stay safely frozen for around 26 hours in an upright freezer, or around 30 hours in a chest freezer, provided the door has not been opened and the freezer is reasonably full. If you think that anything has begun to **DEFROST**, throw it out.

•

Freezers use more energy to keep empty spaces cold, so **FILL GAPS** with loaves of bread or similar basic foods.

FREEZER BURN causes dry, grayish white patches on the surface of frozen food when it is exposed to air. Although the food may have lost a little of its moisture, color, and texture, it should be safe to eat.

•

If you freeze food in a plastic **CONTAINER**, once it has frozen solid, briefly dip the container in hot water to release its contents in a block. Transfer this to a freezer bag, return to the freezer, and the container can be reused.

•

Spirits with an **ALCOHOL** content of 35% or over can be kept in the freezer—this is ideal for those served ice-cold.

Entertaining

Keep party food **BITE-SIZED** and simple, so that guests can eat the food easily with one hand, while holding a glass in the other.

•

When preparing food for a **PICNIC**, make individual pies, quiches, or tartlets, as they are more robust than a slice from a larger pie, quiche, or tart, and more practical, making serving and eating easier.

•

When preparing **PARTY NIBBLES**, use pretzel sticks, short lengths of celery stalks, or sticks cut from large white radishes to pierce **BITE-SIZED** items such as cubes of semi-hard cheese, rolls of Parma ham or prosciutto, beef, or smoked salmon, or cocktail sausages. The whole thing can be eaten and it saves having to dispose of toothpicks (cocktail sticks).

•

When **STEAMING** vegetables, heat the serving dish by inverting it over the steaming basket or pan (it will act as a lid). Remove the dish using an oven mitt, as it will be hot.

•

If you need to **CHILL** a bottle of white or sparkling **WINE** quickly, put it in the freezer for about 30 minutes, but never longer than 45 minutes. Set a timer, otherwise you may forget and end up with an exploded bottle.

WARM up a bottle of red **WINE** by putting it in an ice bucket of warm water (at a temperature of about 68°F/20°C) for 20–30 minutes.

•

Whole star anise will add a rich, spicy flavor to **MULLED WINE**.

•

At **DRINKS PARTIES**, one 75 cl (750 ml) bottle of wine or champagne will give about 6 glasses. Allow at least 2 glasses per person.

•

If you are short of **FRIDGE SPACE**, chill bottles of wine, soft drinks, and water in large plastic boxes (coolers are ideal) or buckets packed with ice, then topped up with cold water.

•

Slice whole fresh strawberries, keeping the slices attached to the green tops, then fan out the slices and use to **DECORATE DESSERTS**.

For extra appeal when making **SANDWICHES**, use a couple of different loaves. For example, use one slice of whole-wheat (wholemeal) and one slice of white bread, or try one slice of rye bread and one slice of mixed-seed bread.

•

Tuck small sprigs of fresh herbs, herb flowers, or garden flowers (tied with ribbon or raffia) into plain **NAPKIN RINGS**. Alternatively, tie freshly cut long chives around rolled-up napkins.

FREEZE AHEAD

Open-freeze slices of **LEMONS**, limes, or oranges on a baking sheet lined with baking parchment. Once solid, transfer to a freezer bag. Add the **FROZEN SLICES** to drinks, as required.

•

Make **ICE CUBES** from different colored fruit juices, then pop into children's party drinks for extra appeal.

•

Freeze small pieces of **FRUIT** in **ICE CUBES** and add them to drinks and cocktails, for extra appeal.

Microwaving

The **MORE** food you are cooking, and the colder it is, the **LONGER** it will take to cook in a microwave.

•

When microwaving items such as **SAUSAGES** or **BACON** that may spit during cooking, cover them loosely with paper towels (kitchen paper), to avoid too much splattering.

•

Some **WHOLE FOODS** such as eggs, potatoes or apples in their skins, (bell) peppers, and sausages should be pricked several times before cooking, otherwise they may burst due to a build-up of **STEAM** under the membrane or skin.

•

Many foods need to be **COVERED** during microwaving. Use microwave-safe plastic wrap (clingfilm), a plate, or a lid. Pierce plastic wrap, or leave a gap at one side if using a plate or lid, to allow excess steam to escape.

•

NEVER operate a microwave oven when it is **EMPTY**, as the microwaves will bounce back to and damage the oven components.

•

Be careful when **STIRRING** heated **LIQUIDS** in a container in the microwave, as they can bubble up without warning.

After food has been **REMOVED** from the microwave, it will continue to cook due to the residual heat within the food, so adhere to **STANDING** times when they are given in recipes.

•

Use a microwave oven with a built-in **TURNTABLE** if possible, and make sure that you turn or stir the food several times during cooking to ensure even cooking throughout. The food toward the **OUTER EDGES** usually cooks first.

•

Take **CARE** when removing the cover from a microwave **CONTAINER** as the steam inside will be very hot.

•

Unless your **MICROWAVE** oven has a broiler (grill) element, the food will not brown during cooking.

•

Microwaved foods can look **PALE** and insipid. Enhance the color of sweet dishes by sprinkling them with **TOASTED** coconut, brown sugar, cinnamon sugar, or ground spices. Frosting (icing) will hide a pale cake. To enhance the color of savory dishes, top with toasted chopped nuts or paprika, brush meat or poultry with a little **SOY SAUCE** or barbecue sauce, or use a basting sauce containing paprika, tomato paste (purée), or mustard.

METAL containers, china with a metallic trim, foil, or crystal glass (which contains lead) should not be used in a microwave. Metal reflects microwaves and may damage the oven components. Microwave-safe plastic containers, ovenproof glass, and ceramic dishes are all suitable, as is most household glazed china. Paper plates and paper towels (kitchen paper) can be used to **REHEAT FOOD** for short periods. Roasting bags (pierced) may be used in a microwave.

•

Cook vegetables in a suitable heatproof serving dish to save on **WASHING UP**.

•

When cooking **CAKES** in a microwave, make sure you only fill the container half full to allow the cake to rise.

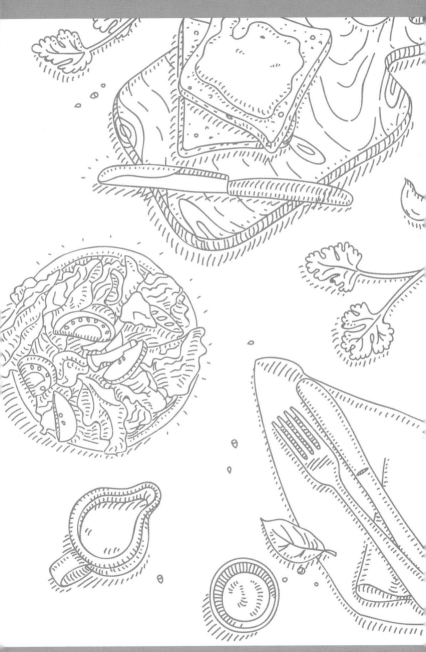

GLOSSARY

Acidulated water
Water with lemon juice or vinegar added. Used to prevent discoloration in some prepared fruit and vegetables.

Al dente
Italian term describing food that is cooked but still has slight resistance or firmness to the bite.

Au gratin
A savory dish sprinkled with breadcrumbs and/or grated cheese and browned under the broiler (grill). Also, a savory dish covered with cheese sauce or grated cheese and baked in the oven.

Bain-marie
A "water bath" used to cook delicate foods such as egg custards and sauces at a constant temperature. The food is placed in a dish over a pan of simmering water, or in a baking pan (tin) half filled with hot water. A double-boiler is also a bain-marie.

Bake blind
To bake an empty pastry shell in a baking pan (tin) before filling. The pastry shell is lined with greaseproof paper, then filled with baking beans to prevent it rising and losing its shape during cooking.

Bard
Thin layers of fat, usually bacon or pork fat, are wrapped or tied around lean cuts of meat, poultry breast meat, or terrines. Barding keeps the meat moist during cooking.

Baste
To spoon cooking juices, melted fat, liquid, or a marinade over food during cooking, to prevent the food drying out and to add flavor.

Beurre manié
Equal quantities of all-purpose (plain) flour and softened butter kneaded together to form a paste, which is used for thickening dishes such as soups, sauces, and stews.

Blanch

To immerse food in boiling water briefly, so it is only partly cooked. Once blanched, the food is plunged into cold water to stop the cooking process. Blanching is used to loosen fruit or vegetable skins or to preserve the color, flavor, texture, and nutrients of vegetables prior to freezing.

Brûlée

French term, meaning "burnt"—a dish with a crisp topping of caramelized sugar.

Chine

To cut through the rib bones of a roast (usually lamb or pork) close to the backbone or spine, or to remove the backbone from a rib roast or rack of meat, to make the meat easier to carve.

Coulis

A smooth sauce (of pouring consistency) that is made by puréeing raw or cooked fruit or cooked vegetables.

Cure

Preserve meat, poultry, or fish by smoking, drying or salting. Curing also adds flavor to food.

Deglaze

To heat liquid, such as stock, water, or wine, with the juices and sediment left in a pan after roasting or sautéing meat or vegetables, stirring and scraping until the sediment has combined with the liquid to make a sauce or gravy.

Disgorge/Degorge

To draw out moisture, extract bitter juices, or remove impurities from food by one of two methods: sprinkling the food with salt and letting it stand, then rinsing and drying it before cooking (for example, eggplants [aubergines] and cucumbers); or soaking the food in water before cooking (for example, meat, offal, fish).

En croûte

Term used to describe food such as fish, meat, or fruit that is wrapped in pastry before baking.

En papillote

Food that is sealed and baked in a parcel of baking parchment or foil. The cooked dish is served from the parcel.

Flambé

To add an alcoholic spirit such as brandy, rum, or whisky to a dish, and then ignite it to burn off the alcohol and add flavor.

Florentine

A savory dish (usually fish or eggs) served with, or containing, spinach, and often cheese sauce.

Fold in

To combine a whisked or creamed mixture by gently cutting into it using a large metal spoon or plastic spatula, to keep as much air as possible in the mixture.

Ganache

A very rich mixture of melted chocolate and cream, which is used as a filling or coating for cakes, pastries, and desserts.

Infuse

To impart flavor into a liquid by adding ingredients such as a vanilla bean (pod), spices, or herbs. The infused liquid is often heated, then left to stand and strained before use.

Julienne

Vegetables, fruit, or citrus zest cut into very fine "matchstick" strips.

Lard

To insert, or thread small strips (lardons) of fat or bacon through the flesh of lean meat, game birds, and poultry using a larding needle, to add succulence and flavor to the meat during roasting.

Liaison

Ingredients used to thicken or bind soups or sauces. Egg yolks, cream, blood, or a combination of ingredients such as flour and water or cream and egg yolks are typical liaisons.

Macerate

To soak raw or dried foods such as fruit in a liquid, such as alcohol or sugar syrup, to soften and flavor the food.

Marinate

To soak or treat raw meat, poultry, or fish in a paste or sauce (usually including oil, wine, lemon juice or vinegar, and other flavorings) to tenderize, flavor, and add moisture.

Pare

To thinly peel the skin or zest from fruit or vegetables.

Punch down (knock back)

To deflate risen yeast dough, in order to disperse the gases created by the fermentation process throughout the dough, to ensure an even texture.

Reduce/reduction

To fast-boil a stock, sauce, or gravy in an uncovered pan, so the liquid reduces to a fraction of its original volume.

The reduction becomes thicker and its flavor more concentrated.

Roux
A mixture of equal amounts of fat (usually butter) and flour cooked together (to different degrees of color) and used to thicken liquids to make sauces or soups.

Rub in
Incorporate fat into flour and other dry ingredients by rubbing the ingredients together using your fingertips, until the mixture resembles breadcrumbs. This creates a short texture used in some pastry, scone, cake, and shortbread recipes.

Sauté
To shallow-fry food in hot melted fat in an uncovered pan over high heat, shaking the pan or tossing the food continuously, until browned all over.

Scald
To pour boiling water over fruit such as tomatoes or peaches to loosen skins. Also, to heat a liquid such as milk until it is just below boiling point.

Seal/sear
To brown meat rapidly all over in hot melted fat before further cooking, to seal in the juices and give it flavor and color.

Steep
To soak food in warm or cold liquid to soften it, to absorb the flavors of the liquid (as from a marinade), or to draw out strong flavors or salt from the food.

Sweat
To cook food, typically sliced or chopped vegetables, gently in a little melted fat or stock, in a covered pan, until the food is soft but not colored or browned.

Temper
To heat then cool chocolate to specific temperatures, to make it easier to use and to produce a glossy finish when it sets.

Truss
To tie or skewer poultry, game birds, or boned joints of meat into a neat shape before cooking.

Index

Acknowledgments

I would like to thank Penny Craig at Ryland Peters & Small for approaching me and asking me to write this book, and for her continued support throughout this project. I would also like to thank Sarah Vaughan for her editing, and Geoff Borin for his creative design. Finally, my special thanks go to my husband, Robbie, for his ongoing support and encouragement with this book.